Southam Parish Land Processioning 1747-1784

Goochland, Cumberland, and Powhatan Counties Virginia

Ann K. Blomquist

WILLOW BEND BOOKS

2013

WILLOW BEND BOOKS
AN IMPRINT OF HERITAGE BOOKS, INC.

Books, CDs, and more—Worldwide

For our listing of thousands of titles see our website
at
www.HeritageBooks.com

Published 2013 by
HERITAGE BOOKS, INC.
Publishing Division
100 Railroad Ave. #104
Westminster, Maryland 21157

Other Heritage Books by the author:
Goochland County, Virginia Court Order Books 1 and 2, 1728–1731
Goochland County, Virginia Court Order Book 3, 1731–1735
Goochland County, Virginia Court Order Book 4, 1735–1741
Goochland County, Virginia Court Order Book 5, 1741–1745
*Southam Parish Land Processioning, 1747–1784
Goochland, Cumberland, and Powhatan Counties, Virginia*
The Vestry Book of Southam Parish, Cumberland County, Virginia, 1745–1792
The Vestry Book of South Farnham Parish, Essex County, Virginia, 1739–1779

International Standard Book Numbers
Paperbound: 978-1-58549-932-8
Clothbound: 978-0-7884-6910-7

Contents

INTRODUCTION

This book contains abstracts of the land processioning orders and returns for Southam Parish for the years 1747 through 1784 while Southam Parish was part of the counties of Goochland, Cumberland, and Powhatan. The original information is found in the Vestry Book of Southam Parish which contains the detailed records of the parish business for the years 1745-1792. This volume is intended to be a companion book to the complete Vestry Book of Southam Parish.

Processioning

Parish business was conducted by the church vestrymen who were responsible for providing the community with a minister and readers, churches and chapels, care for the poor, and the processioning of property.

Land processioning was an important activity. Throughout the colony of Virginia, land was processioned every four years to determine the bounds of every landholder's property. The vestrymen divided the parish into precincts of convenient size with several men appointed to conduct the processioning for each precinct. The returns were recorded in the vestry book.

Though processioning in Virginia had been sporadic and incomplete in the early years, by the time Southam Parish was created in 1745, processioning was well established and regular. Vestrymen understood the process and generally followed the procedures.

The value of the Southam Parish vestry book lies in the dual presence of processioning orders stating the precinct boundaries plus the returns with the names of the landowners within each precinct. The processioning orders give quite good descriptions of the precinct boundaries using creeks, rivers, roads, and properties. This allows a fairly accurate location of the precinct to be established. If a precinct return with names was recorded, then the location of a landowner or a family can be at least be narrowed to a precinct. If either part of the combination is lacking, then the location of a landowner cannot be identified. For example, the Vestry Book of St. Paul's Parish includes detailed returns and numbered precincts, but no boundaries.[1] So the location of the landowners is approximate at best.

The processioning records for Southam Parish comprise over 60% of the vestry book. The orders were usually given by the vestry in the fall of one year with the returns due by the spring of the next year. The returns include the names of the landowners who participated in the processioning process. Unfortunately, some returns are not complete, and in some years, were not made at all.

The conclusion of the American Revolution brought dramatic changes in some governmental institutions including the disestablishment of the Anglican Church. Freedom of worship meant no government-supported parishes. Processioning continued but served as a means of reducing property line disputes.

Southam Parish

When Southam Parish was created in January 1745, it was completely contained within Goochland County, lying in the section of the county south of the James River. St. James Northam was the parish serving the Goochland residents north of the James River. In 1749, Southam Parish residents wished to have their civil government separate from Goochland, so Cumberland County was formed and coincided with Southam Parish. As the population increased and desired services closer to home, the residents in the western section of Cumberland requested a separate parish. In 1772, Littleton Parish was removed from Southam. This reduced Southam Parish to its eastern half. Using the established dividing line between Southam and Littleton parishes to also divide the counties, the residents of Southam Parish were granted a new county, Powhatan, in 1777.

The following chart shows the changes to Southam Parish:

Year	Parish	County
1728	St. James Parish	Goochland County
1745	Southam Parish	Goochland County
1749	Southam Parish	Cumberland County
1772	Southam Parish (Littleton removed)	Cumberland County
1777	Southam Parish	Powhatan County

While Southam Parish was undergoing its various changes, there was another parish existing in the area. French Huguenot refugees had settled at Manakintown in 1700 and were permitted to form their own parish, King William Parish. Their land bounded the northeast corner of Southam Parish along the James River and the boundary with Chesterfield County. The processioning records often mention King William Parish or "the French line." This section of the county was consistently omitted in the Southam processioning orders and returns. The law which created King William Parish did not clearly identify its location or boundaries. So, modern researchers cannot be certain where the boundaries of King William Parish were exactly located. The possibilities include modern County Road (CR) 711 and CR 635, or CR 711 and Dutoy Creek, or CR 711 and Bernard's Creek, or some other arrangement. I have selected CR 711 and Dutoy Creek.

For 1745-1772 while it was in Goochland and Cumberland counties, Southam Parish covered about 560 square miles, but was reduced to about 260 square miles for 1772-1792 when it was in Cumberland and Powhatan counties.

There are two small differences between original Southam Parish and the combination map of current Cumberland and Powhatan counties. The original county line between Cumberland and Albemarle was completely straight.[2] In 1778, a small piece of then Buckingham County was added back to Cumberland.[3] In a similar manner, the original line between Cumberland and Chesterfield counties was straight. In 1850, long after Southam Parish ceased, a small piece of Chesterfield County was transferred to Powhatan County.[4]

Processioning Precincts

Because Southam Parish was created in January 1745, its first processioning was 1747. The processioning years were 1747, 1751, 1755, 1759, 1763, 1771, 1775, 1779, and 1783. The returns were recorded the next year, so these returns are dated 1748, 1756, 1760, 1765, 1772, and 1780. No returns were recorded for 1752, 1776, or 1784. There are no processioning records for 1767.

The precincts are not numbered in the vestry book but were assigned by the compiler based on their order in the vestry book. The precinct order often follows a pattern. In 1747, the precincts were generally arranged from east to west, while for 1751 through 1771, they were arranged from west to east. There is no particular order for the final three processionings although it remained fixed for all three.

As the population and number of landowners increased in Southam Parish, the number of precincts rose from 34 to 43 over the first 24 years. The size and shape of the precincts varied greatly. In 1747, #23 was the smallest while nearby #34 was comparatively large. Perhaps the vestrymen were dissatisfied with their arrangement of #34 because by the next processioning, it was separated into 3 precincts. Precinct #27 (1747) was uncharacteristically long and narrow. Interestingly, 12 of the original 34 precincts retained their boundaries throughout the life of the parish with precincts #11 and #12 combined into one until 1771 when it returned to its original two.[5]

The goal of the 1772 division of Southam was to create two parishes with a fairly equal number of tithables. In the first processioning after Littleton was formed, the number of precincts in Southam dropped to 19 where it remained until the parish ceased to exist.

The following chart summarizes the number of precincts, the number of returns, and the percent of returns.

Year	# Precincts	# Returns	% Returns
1747	34	21	62%
1751	35	9 full, 6 partial	17%
1755	40	21	54%
1759	41	14	34%
1763	41	33	80%
1771	43	6	14%
1775	19	0	0%
1779	19	9	47%
1784	19	0	0%

The boundaries of the 19 precincts of Southam Parish after Littleton Parish was removed in 1772 remained the same for the processionings of 1775, 1779, and 1783. Since these processionings were taking place during the upheaval of the American Revolution, it is not surprising that the returns are disappointing. There are no returns at all for 1775 and 1783, while 1779 was only 47% complete.

Parish Landmarks

Roads and waterways were the primary features that were needed for the mapping of the parish precincts. For the most part, the paths of roads that exist today were cut in colonial times. Many roadbeds have remained the same for three hundred years because they have continued to be convenient over the years. However, when roads were no longer useful, they were abandoned and new ones were created.

Not only have most roadbeds remained stable, but many of their names are unchanged. Ancient Buckingham Road still exists in sections. Old Buckingham Road ran parallel to the Appomattox River, turning northward to Scottsville (now Powhatan) and east into Chesterfield County. The old Cumberland Courthouse Road joined Chapel Road to continue on to Buckingham Road just west of Scottsville. The construction of U.S. Highway 60 used the best of both of these old paths. Highway 60 follows the Cumberland Courthouse Road to Powhatan and then runs close to old Buckingham Road but straightens out for fast modern traffic. The modern highway takes travelers through both county seats of Cumberland Courthouse and Powhatan.

There were some parish features with unusual names. Tear Wallet, which evolved into Tare Wallet and Tar Wallet, has a interesting variety of sources, all of which begin with an animal tearing into the food bags of humans. One version has a hog drover napping under the trees who awakens to a hog rooting through his "wallet," a food bag in earlier time. He chased the hog away, hollering, "I'll teach you to tear into my wallet!"[6] Negro's Arm Road appeared even on the 1858 and 1880 maps, but is now Academy Road (CR 603). There is no known history for this intriguing name.[7] Soakass Creek of 1759 is now Bear Creek. Wouldn't we like to know how the creek got this name.

The churches and individual landowners were also mentioned in the precinct orders. Peterville Church, Worley's Chapel (also called South Chapel), and Tar Wallet Chapel all have identifiable locations. However, Ham Chapel has not existed for many years and its location is only estimated through these parish records. The location of some landowners can be closely approximated when their properties are named in the precinct boundaries.

Though there were no accurate colonial maps of the area, the residents had a clear idea of the lay of the land. The processioning orders and returns indicate that the vestrymen and the landowners knew the features of the parish and exactly where everything was located. Though some descriptions seem incomplete or vague, we appreciate the overall completeness of these processioning records.

Maps of the Parish

Though these maps will not necessarily pinpoint the location of the land of our ancestors, they will help identify the section of the county and the neighbors.

To draw the processioning precincts, it was necessary to locate the creeks, rivers, and roads of the parish. The earliest maps for the area were sought. The ideal map to use for drawing the precincts would be a detailed contemporary colonial map. But no such document was probably ever created.

In 1777 when the creation of Powhatan County from Cumberland County was anticipated, a map was prepared probably to accompany the petition to the Virginia General Assembly. This map is one of the earliest county maps in the collection of the Library of Virginia. This 1777 map of Cumberland County, unfortunately, includes only a few creeks and rivers. Though the bridges are enumerated, no roads were drawn. A dotted line labeled "parish line" shows the successful separation between Littleton Parish and Southam Parish. This was used to also divide the two counties. There are no other known early maps of the Cumberland County portion of Southam Parish.

In 1858, a map of Powhatan County was drawn by two Virginia Military Institute cadets. While this map has roads, creeks, and rivers drawn and named, it is rather incorrect in its proportions, curvature of the creeks, and location of the roads.

In 1864, both Cumberland and Powhatan were surveyed under the direction of Maj. Gen. Jeremy F. Gilmer of the Confederate War Department. These fine maps include details such as residences, churches, names of roads and waterways. The Gilmer Powhatan map is slightly difficult to read. The collection of Gilmer maps is now located at the Virginia Historical Society and copies can be purchased there.

In 1878, the Powhatan County Court commissioned Joseph E. LaPrade (1845-1903) to survey and map the county showing the roads, distances, water courses, public places, and principal residences.[8] Completed in 1880, this map is important because it is an accurate map of the county and, for our purposes, it shows the county before significant changes in the roads were brought on by the use of automobiles. Comparing this map with the 1858 map shows little new road development. This survey was completed after the Civil War and shortly after Reconstruction, so there would have been few changes even since parish times. The only technological advance is the railroad track through the lower southeast corner of the county.

In current times, the Virginia Department of Transportation publishes General Highway Maps of every Virginia county which identify waterways, roads, churches, cemeteries, and other important features. By combining the county maps for Cumberland and Powhatan, a modern map of Southam Parish could be created.

Some of these maps are included in this book.

Abstracts of the Processioning Records

These abstracts are arranged in the following order: the precinct number; the boundaries with the page number from the vestry book of the processioning orders; the processioners; the landowners in alphabetical order with the page number of the return. Boundaries are usually clockwise or counterclockwise around the precinct; however, sometimes there is no particular order.

The processioning orders include the expressions "up" and "down" for the creeks and roads. In this context, up means westward and down means eastward because the eastern part of the county was geographically lower. The James and Appomattox Rivers both flowed from west to east, so up meant upriver and down was down river.

There are no numbers for the precincts in the original Vestry Book. The precincts have been numbered consecutively as the orders appear in the vestry book. To aid the reader in locating the original description of the processioning precinct, the page number is given in brackets [xx]. The returns were not recorded in the corresponding order to the precinct orders. If a return for the precinct was recorded, its page number in the original book is also noted in brackets.

Editorial Notes and Method

After numerous trials with all of the available maps, the best map for 1745-1772 Southam Parish was a combination of the 1864 Gilmer Cumberland County map and the 1880 LaPrade Powhatan County map. For 1772-1792 Southam Parish, the 1880 LaPrade Powhatan County map was the best. Originally, I marked the precincts in colors, but that proved impractical for publication. For this book, the precincts are numbered and marked along their boundaries. King William Parish is also identified. There are separate maps for the first 6 processionings, but only one was needed for the final 3 processionings because the precincts did not change.

Though most of the pieces seem to finally fit, the final drawing of the precincts certainly may be incorrect. Ancient and variable names of colonial landmarks makes definite identification of some shared boundaries between precincts uncertain. The problem precincts are noted for each processioning. Occasionally there were obvious errors in the vestry records which I have noted.

When I first considered mapping the Southam Parish precincts, I anticipated that it would be an impossible task. I had no expectation of being able to successfully map the parish. Beginning with 1747, out of the first 6 precincts, only the first one was plotted with any confidence. My initial pessimism seemed confirmed. But with persistence, names became familiar, edges began to match, and the pieces of the parish puzzle began to fit. It was a wonderful surprise when the maps seemed to work and were finally finished.

August, 2003   Ann Kicker Blomquist
Orlando, Florida

ENDNOTES

1. Chamberlayne, C. G.
2. 5 Hening 266-267.
3. 9 Hening 559.
4. Acts of the VA General Assembly, 1849 and 1850, Chapter 28, p 26.
5. Original precincts #1, 5, 6, 8, 10, 14, 16, 17, 18, 19, 21, 22. Their numbers changed but not the boundaries.
6. Hopkins, p 25; Vaughan, p 69.
7. Couture, p 339.
8. Couture, p 467, 468.

****

Illustration from *Colonial Living*
by Edwin Tunis

The Precinct Maps

of

Southam Parish

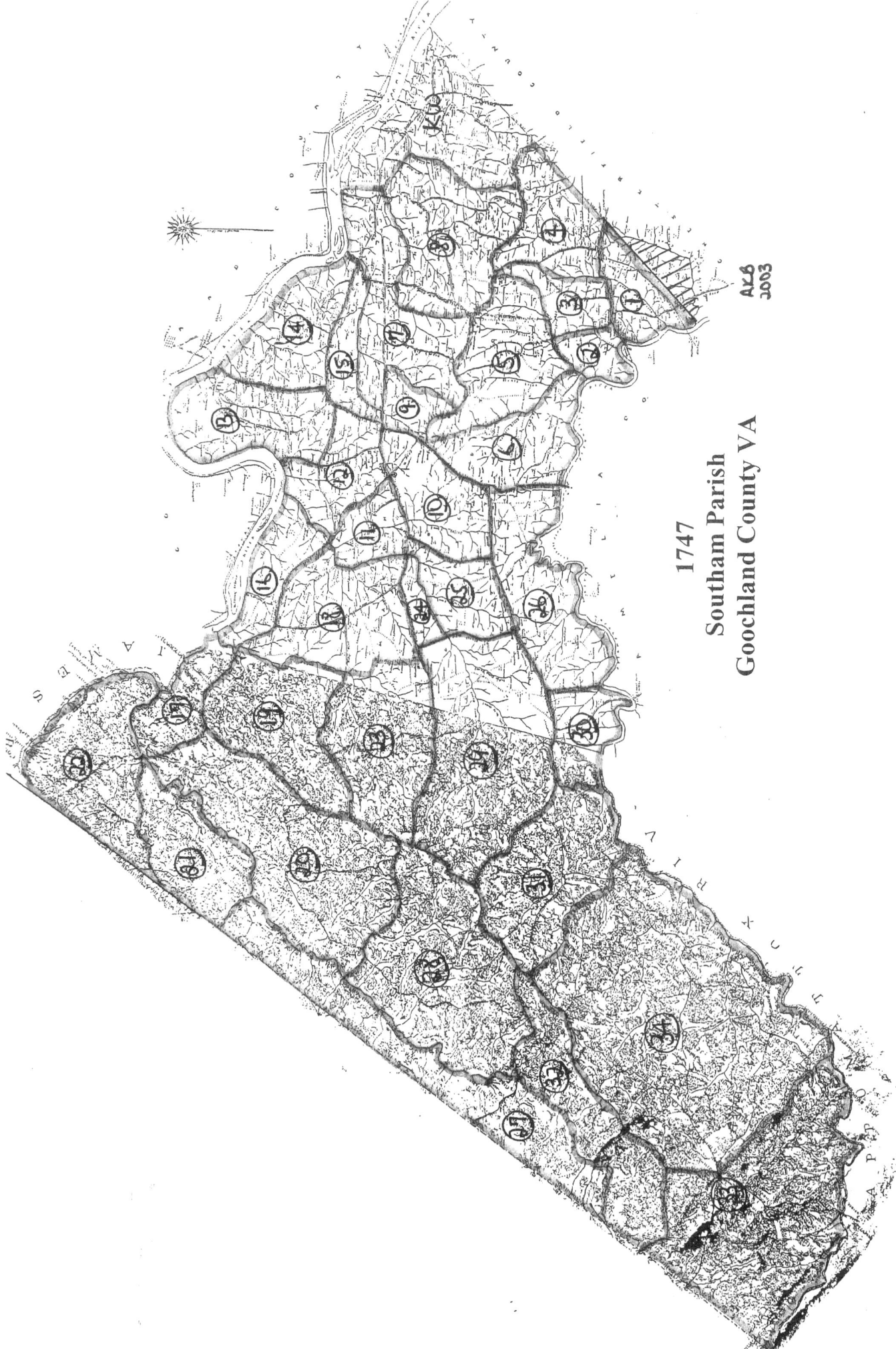

1747
Southam Parish
Goochland County VA

ALB
2003

1747 Goochland County in Southam Parish

This the first processioning conducted for the new Southam Parish. The orders are dated July 27, 1747, pages [10-22], and the returns May 21, 1748, pages [25-38]. Of the 34 precincts, 21 reported full returns for a return rate of 62%. Shared borders between some precincts are uncertain: between #3 and #4, between #26 and #30, between #30 and #31.

Precinct #1
Boundaries: Begin at the County line at Appomattox River, up Genito Road to Appomattox River, down Appomattox River [10]
Landowners: Perrin Alday, William Bass, Lodowick Elam, Margaret Hancock, Creed Haskins, Gideon Lockett, Joel Lockett, Thomas Lockett, Francis Marshall, William Marshall, Arthur Moseley, Benjamin Moseley, Richard Moseley, John Northcut, John Timson deceased, George Todd deceased, George Williamson [31]
Processioners: William Marshall, Arthur Moseley, William Moseley

Precinct #2
Boundaries: Begin at Genito Road at Butterwood Creek, up the Road to the Appomattox River, up the River to Fighting Creek, up the Creek to William Clay, down Clay's Path by Edward Watkins [10]
Processioners: Richard Moseley, Francis Marshall, Thomas Lockett
Landowners: Col. Banley, Thomas Hall, Joel Lockett, John Patson, Richard Randolph, John Stort, Timson, Edward Watkins, George Williamson [36]

Precinct #3
Boundaries: Begin at William Clay's on Fighting Creek, up the Creek to Buckingham Road at the Reading Place (Worley's Chapel), down Buckingham Road to Thomas Watkins, down Butterwood Creek to the Main [Genito] Road, up by Edward Watkins to William Clay [11]
Processioners: Henry Clay, William Clay, John Moseley
Landowners: Francis Cheatham, Henry Clay, William Clay, John Farmer, Steven Mallet, John Moseley, William Riggin, Merry Roberts, Morris Roberts, Timson, Edward Watkins, Thomas Watkins, John Worley, William Worley [26]

Precinct #4
Boundaries: Begin at Buckingham Road at the head of Butterwood Creek, down Buckingham Road to the County line, along the line to Genito Road, up Genito Road to Butterwood Creek, up the Creek [11]
Processioners: John Watkins, Joseph Baugh, Israel Winfrey

Landowners: William Akin, William Bass, James Baugh, Joseph Baugh, Thomas Baugh, Francis Cheatham, Thomas Cheatham, James Chitwood, Mathew Chitwood, Henry Clay, Lodowick Elam, John Farmer, Henry Hatcher, Josiah Hatcher, Joel Lockett, Arthur Mosley, Benjamin Mosley, John Mosley, Morris Roberts, Stephen Russell, Thomas Russell, Edward Watkins, John Watkins, Thomas Watkins, Israel Winfree, John Wooldridge, Thomas Wooldridge, William Worley [27]

Precinct #5

Boundaries: Begin at the Fork of Fighting Creek, up Randolph's Fork to Buckingham Road, down Buckingham Road to the Road to the Reading Place (Worley's), down Clay's Fork [11]

Processioners: Richard Povall, George Williamson, John Mossom

Landowners: Henry Clay, James Davis, John Dunkin (Duncan), John Hale, Thomas Hall, Samuel Hatcher, Richard Ligon, John Mosley, John Mossom, Richard Povall, John Radford, Richard Randolph, William Randolph, William Riggin, Philip Thomas, Abraham Womack [33]

Precinct #6

Boundaries: Begin at the mouth of Fighting Creek, up the Appomattox River to Lyle's Ford, along Lyle's Road to Benjamin Childrey, down Buckingham Road to Fighting Creek, down the Creek [12]

Processioners: Benjamin Childrey, Henry Brazeal, Phillip Thomas

Landowners: no list of owners presented, only the statement "processioned all the lands except Nicholas Giles" [32]

Precinct #7

Boundaries: Begin at the mouth of Fine Creek, down the [James] River to the French line to Jones Creek, up the Creek to the head, to the nearest course to Buckingham Road, up the Road to Stratton's House, down Fine Creek to the beginning [12]

Processioners: John Cannefax, Nathaniel Maxey, Bennett Goode

Landowners: John Archer, John Baskerville, Joseph Bondurant, John Cannifax, George Carrington, James Davis, Peter Jefferson, Richard Ligon, Walter Maxey, Daniel Mayo, Mrs. Mayo, John Mossom, John Pleasant, William Randolph deceased, John Radford, James Robinson, Thomas Turpin, Abraham Womack, Abraham Womack Jr [34]

Precinct #8

Boundaries: Begin at the south side of Jones Creek at the French line, up the creek to the head, to the nearest course to Buckingham Road, down Buckingham Road to the road to the

French line, along that line to the beginning [12]

Processioners: John Radford, William Maxey, Sylvanus Maxey

Landowners: Matthew Agee, Thomas Bassett, John Bondurant, Peter Bondurant, Thomas Bradley, James Cocke, Richard Epperson, Samuel Hatcher, Esther Landson, John Maxey, Nathaniel Maxey, Radford Maxey, Sylvanus Maxey, Walter Maxey, William Maxey, John Mossom, John Radford, William Riggin, John Smith, Joseph Suinne, Jacob Tribue, Thomas Turpin, John Worley [28]

Precinct #9

Boundaries: Begin at Stratton's plantation, up Buckingham Road to Benjamin Childrey, along the Courthouse Road to Chandler, down Chapel Road to Fine Creek at Three Bridges, up the Creek to the beginning [13]

Processioners: John Baskerville, William Chandler, Anthony Hughes

Landowners: John Bakserville, Joseph Chandler, William Chandler, Benjamin Childrey, James Davis, former Glebe, Anthony Hughes, James Ligon, Matthew Ligon, Richard Ligon, Daniel Mayo, Miss Mayo, William Randolph, William Randolph deceased, Stratton, Philip Thomas, Charles Woodson [26]

Precinct #10

Boundaries: Begin at Benjamin Childrey, along the Courthouse Road to Lax, up the Chapel Road to the Ridge Path between Little Deep Creek and Great Deep Creek, along the Path to Buckingham Road, down the road to the beginning [13]

Processioners: Thomas Walker, Thomas Stovall, John Legrand

Landowners: no return recorded

Precinct #11

Boundaries: Begin at Deep Creek, up the Main Fork to the Chapel Road, down the Road to the new road at Walton's, along the new road to Askew's Path, up the Path to River Road, up River Road to the beginning [13]

Processioners: Joel Chandler, John Taylor, William Taylor

Landowners: Stephen Bedford, Joel Chandler, Phillip Cockaham, Nicholas Cox, Allen Howard, William Hunt, John Lake, William Lax, Thomas Low, Ann Mayo, Jacob Mosby, Abraham Salley, John Hyde Saunders, John Scott, John Taylor, William Taylor, Robert Walton [37]

Precinct #12

Boundaries: Begin at the mouth of Deep Creek, up the Creek to the Bridge, down the [River] Road to Askew's Path, down Askew's Path to the new road, along the new road to Walton, down to the Chapel Road to Lax, along the Courthouse Road to Bates, up the River Road to Solomon's Creek, down the creek to the James River, up the River to the beginning [14]

Processioners: John Hyde Saunders, William Lax, David Johnson

Landowners: James Bates, John Bates, Capt Bedford, Major Charton, Joel Chandler, William Chandler, Thomas Dickens, Dudley Diggs, John Franklin, Major Howard, William Hunt, Anthony Hughes, Daniel Johnson, John Leak, Mrs. Mayo, John Pleasant, Mrs. Randolph, John Hyde Saunders, John Scott [Chsot], Bartholomew Stovall, John Taylor, William Taylor, Edmond Toney, Robert Walton, Charles Woodson [30]

Precinct #13

Boundaries: Begin at the mouth of Solomon's Creek, down the James River to Jacob Michaux's Ferry, along Ferry Road to Bates, up the [River] road to Solomon's Creek, down the creek to the beginning [14]

Processioners: Paul Michaux, Daniel Coleman, Frederick Cox

Landowners: no list of owners presented, only the failures: James Bates, Thomas Dickens deceased, Dudley Diggs [31]

Precinct #14

Boundaries: Begin at Jacob Michaux's Ferry, along the Ferry Road to Bates' house, down the [River] road to Fine Creek, down the creek to the [James] River, up the [James] River to the beginning [14]

Processioners: Robert Hughes, Charles Railey, Joseph Johnson

Landowners: Salvater Alford, Henry Bagby, John Cannon, Frederick Cox, John Cox, William Dudley, John Fleming, John Fleming Jr, Francis James, Susannah Gasper, Joseph Hughes, Robert Hughes, Stephen Hughes, Joseph Johns, Jacob Michaux's orphans, John Pleasant, William Reynolds, Charles Riley, James Riley, John Riley, John Robinson, John Spaulding, John Spurlock, Daniel Stoner, Nicholas Wilkinson, Daniel Wilmore, Stephen Woodson deceased [33]

Precinct #15

Boundaries: Begin at the road where it crosses Fine Creek at Scott's Mill, up the Road to Bates, along the road to Lax, down the Chapel Road to Fine Creek at the Three Bridges, down the creek to the beginning [15]

Processioners: John Bates, Bartholomew Stovall, Daniel Wilmore

Landowners: Thomas Bassett, Charles Bates, William Chandler, James Glass, Samuel Mansfield, Ann Mayo, Christopher Nordin, John Pleasants, Major Stoner, Daniel Wilmore, Charles Woodson, Elizabeth Woodson [26]

Precinct #16
Boundaries: Begin at Deep Creek Bridge, down the creek to the [James] River, up the River to Muddy Creek, up the Creek to the bridge, down the Main Road to the beginning [15]
Processioners: Alexander Moss, Abraham Womack Jr, John Alexander
Landowners: John Alexander, John Bradley, Miles Gathwrite, George Going, Robert Hughes, Robert Hughes Jr, Alexander Moss, Micajah Mosby, Thomas Moss, George Owen, John Pleasants, Jane Randolph, Drury Scruggs, Abraham Womack [36]

Precinct #17
Boundaries: Begin at Muddy Creek Bridge, down the creek to the River, up the James River to Willis River, up Willis River to the bridge, down the Main Road to the beginning [15]
Processioners: Robert Carter, Isaac Hughes, William Dillon
Landowners: incomplete return only naming Major Bolling, Thomas Bracket, George Carrington, Robert Carter Jr, Nicholas Davies, Henry Dillon, William Dillon, Robert Hughes [32]

Precinct #18
Boundaries: Begin at Deep Creek Bridge, up the Creek to the Chapel Road, up the Road and Scotts Path to Muddy Creek, down the creek to the River Road, down the River Road to the beginning [16]
Processioners: William Moss Sr, Miles Gathwrite, Abraham Womack Sr
Landowners: no returns recorded because Abraham Womack was deceased, Miles Gathwrite moved to Henrico County, though William Moss states he attended [38]

Precinct #19
Boundaries: Begin at Muddy Creek Bridge, up the River Road to the Widow Dillon's Path, by Salmon's to Ham Chapel, by the new Chapel Road near Mr. Scott to Muddy Creek, down the said creek to the beginning [16]
Processioners: Thomas Walton, John Creasy, William Palmer
Landowners: no list of owners returned, only failures: John Blevins, Bowler Cocke, Nicholas Davies, Benjamin Dumas, Rachel Ferris, Benjamin Harrison, Toliac Powers, William Willis [37]

Precinct #20
Boundaries: Begin at Widow Dillon's Path, by Salmon's to Ham Chapel, by Pruet's Path to Barnet's Road, by the said Road to Willis River, down the River to the Bridge, down the River Road to the beginning [16]
Processioners: James Cunningham, Merry Webb, John Salmon
Landowners: no return recorded

Precinct #21
Boundaries: Begin at Willis Bridge, up Willis River to Randolph's Creek, up the creek to the county line, along the line to the River Road, down the road to the beginning [17]
Processioners: Samuel Bridgewater, Joseph Price, Valentine Martin
Landowners: Thomas Bassett, George Carrington, James Cunningham, William Cunningham, Phineas Glover, Edward Hambleton, Stephen Hughes, Gideon Martin, Valentine Martin, Joseph Price, John Reynolds [32]

Precinct #22
Boundaries: Begin at Willis Bridge, down Willis River to James River, up James River to the county line, along the line to the River Road, down the road to the beginning [17]
Processioners: Joseph Hooper, Samuel Taylor, Phineas Glover
Landowners: Isaac Bates, Thomas Bracket, John Burnet, George Carrington, Robert Carter, James Daniel, Phineas Glover, Benjamin Harrison, Joseph Hooper, Phillip Mayo, Cornelius Nevil, James Nevil, David Prior, Skelton, Richard Taylor, Henry Trent [35]

Precinct #23
Boundaries: Begin at Ham Chapel, by the new [Chapel] Road near Mr. Scott, to Muddy Creek, up the creek to Barnet's Road, up Barnet's Road to Pruet's Path, along the path to Ham Chapel [17]
Processioners: John Merryman, William Bond, Thomas Watts
Landowners: William Bond, Thomas Carter, William Cox, Robert Douglas, Joel Fain, Richard Fain, Sampson Fleming, Ralph Flippen, Thomas Flippen, Peter Holland, John Hudgins, Phillip Hudgins, John Hudson, Ashford Hughes, Orlando Hughes, Joel Meadows, John Merryman, William Mullins, George Owen, Phillip Poindexter, David Roberts, William Salmon, Robert Walton, Thomas Walton, Thomas Watson, Jacob Winfrey, Sylvanus Witt [25]

Precinct #24
Boundaries: Begin at Great Deep Creek Bridge at [Chapel] Road, up the Creek to Mrs. Mayo's Mill, by her Chair Road to the Chapel Road, down the Chapel Road to the beginning [18]
Processioners: George Stovall, Hezekiah Mosby, William Roberts
Landowners: only the following names returned: Benjamin Mosby, James Roberts, William Roberts, Francis Steger, George Stovall [37]

Precinct #25
Boundaries: Begin at Great Deep Creek Bridge at the Chapel Road, down the Road to the Ridge Path, the Path to Buckingham Road, up the Road to Benjamin Harris, by his path to

Mrs. Mayo's upper mill, down the creek to the beginning [18]

Processioners: Philip Poindexter, William Smith, John Cardwell

Landowners: Capt. Barnes, Joel Chandler, Benjamin Harris, John Hughes, Gervas Jackson, John Phelps, John Reddiford, Francis Steger, William Stone, David Winifred, Joseph Woodson [37]

Precinct #26

Boundaries: Begin at Lyles' Ford, along the Courthouse Road to Benjamin Childrey, up Buckingham Road to the Two Blazed Path, along the Path to the [Appomattox] River, down the River to the beginning [18]

Processioners: William Stone, Joseph Woodson, Samuel Burton

Landowners: George Baskerville, Hutchins Burton, Benjamin Childrey, James Cocke, Stephen Cox, Nathaniel Maxey, William Shays, Phillip Thomas, John Woodson, John Wright [31]

Precinct #27

Boundaries: Begin at the mouth of Randolph's Creek, up the creek to the county line, along the line to Brooks' Mill, down Willis' River to the beginning [19]

Processioners: Robert Burton, Hutchins Burton, William Spiers

Landowners: possibly incomplete return naming only Thomas Bassett, Isaac Bates, Mr. Bell, Hutchins Burton, Robert Burton, Walter Daniel, Joseph Farrar, William Finney, Benjamin Harrison, Drury Scruggs, William Spears, Robert Wooding [33]

Precinct #28

Boundaries: Begin at Quarter [?], up Willis River to Buckingham Road, down the Road to Daniels, down Daniels new Road to Johns, up Hornquarter Road to Barnet's Fork, up Barnet's Road to the beginning [19]

Processioners: Richard Burton, Josiah Burton, Samuel Allen Jr, William Johns

Landowners: no return recorded

Precinct #29

Boundaries: Begin at Johns, up the new Road to Buckingham Road, Buckingham Road to Benjamin Harris, by his path to Mrs. Mayo's upper Mill, by her Chair Road to the Chapel Road, up the same to the beginning [19]

Processioners: John Robinson, John Hobson, John Scruggs

Landowners: no return recorded

Precinct #30
Boundaries: Begin at the Two Blazed Path on Appomattox River, up the path [error, should be Appomattox River] to McCoy's, by Burton's Path to Buckingham Road, down the Road to the Two Blazed Path, along the path to the beginning [19]
Processioners: Stephen Cox, Richard Parker, Adolphus Hendrick
Landowners: Patrick Adams, Hutchins Burton, Samuel Burton, George Cox, Henry Cox, Stephen Cox, Holman Freeman, David Hadaway, Benjamin Harris, Henry Hatcher, Isaac Hughes, James Murray, Richard Parker, Daniel Terry, Robert Thompson, William Shay [27]

Precinct #31
Boundaries: Begin at McCoy's on Appomattox River, by Burton's Path to Buckingham Road, up the Road to Daniels, up Randolph's Road to Tear Wallet Creek, down the creek and Great Guinea Creek to the River, down the River to the beginning [20]
Processioners: John Woodson, Joseph Terry, Thomas Davenport
Landowners: "no person attended us" [38]

Precinct #32
Boundaries: Begin at Daniels, up Buckingham Road to Willis River, up the River to Brooks Mill, down the Road to the beginning [20]
Processioners: Thomas Harvey, Williams Daniel, William Trigg
Landowners: John Archer, Archibald Cary, William Chumles, Daniel Coleman, Colquitt, Williams Daniel, James Daniels, James Doudy, William Easley, Warham Easley, Ralph Flipping, Thomas Harvey, Adolphus Hendrick, Benjamin Hendrick, Thomas Johns, Robert Kent, John Martin, William Mills, Josiah Payne, John Retterford, Alexander Spears, William Still, Henry Terry, Alexander Trent, William Trigg [30]

Precinct #33
Boundaries: Begin at Brooks Mill, along the county line to Appomattox River, down the River to Green Creek, up the Creek to Randolph's Road, down the Road to Brooks Road, up the Road to the beginning [20]
Processioners: John Cooke, John Brown, Richard Ward
Landowners: no return recorded

Precinct #34
Boundaries: Begin at Tear Wallet Bridge, down the same and Great Guinea to Appomattox River, up the River to Green Creek, up the Creek to Randolph's Road, down the Road to the beginning [21]
Processioners: William Womack, Daniel Coleman Jr, Charles Bostick, Gideon Glenn
Landowners: "no person attended to show the lines" [38]

EVERYDAY CLOTHES

Illustrations from *Shaw's Fortune*
by Edwin Tunis

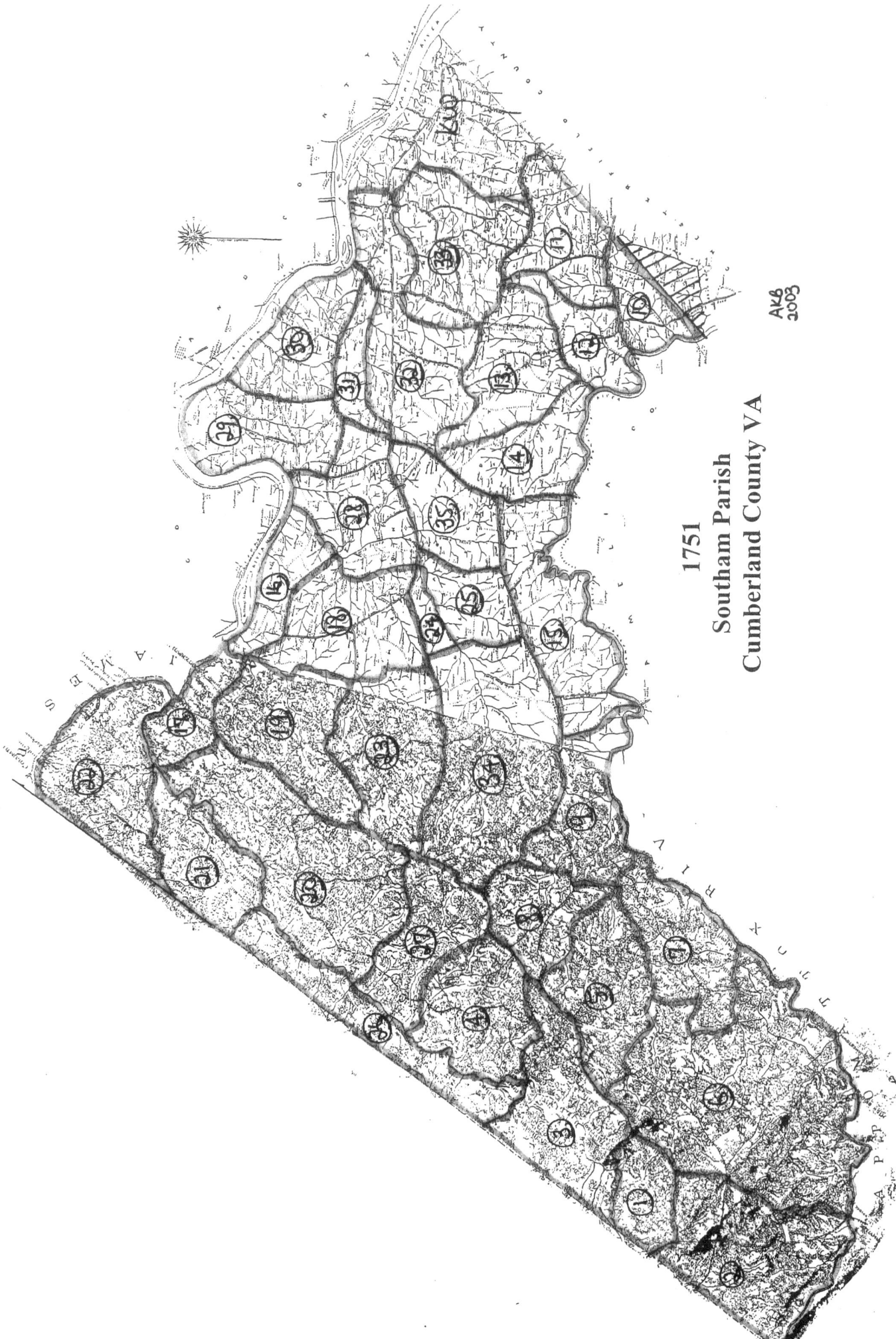

1751
Southam Parish
Cumberland County VA

AKB
2003

1751 Cumberland County

This the second processioning conducted for Southam Parish. The orders are dated September 10, 1751, pages [53-58], and the returns May 16, 1752, pages [63-69]. Of the 35 precincts, only 6 reported full returns for a return rate of 17%. Nine additional precincts provided vague returns with statements such as "we have processioned and renewed all of the lines within our precinct mentioned in the order."

Precinct #1
Boundaries: Begin at the county line on Brook's Road, along the line to Bollings Road, down to the Main Road, up the same to the beginning [53]
Processioners: John Retterford, William Retterford, Robert Thomson

Precinct #2
Boundaries: All the lands between Brookes and Randolph's Roads up to the county line, [and the Appomattox River] [53]
Processioners: George Wright, Charles Anderson, John Richason

Precinct #3
Boundaries: All the lands between the County Line, Bowlings Road, Buckingham Road, and the main county road [53]
Processioners: Williams Daniel, William Mills, William Trigg
Landowners: "this order came too late, please excuse your humble servant" [62]

Precinct #4
Boundaries: All the lands between Buckingham Road and Harrison's Road, down to Johns Road, [and Willis River] [53]
Processioners: Samuel Allen, Alexander Trent, Thomas Coleman
Landowners: John Allen, Samuel Allen, James Anderson, David Bell, John Bradley, Archibald Cary, Daniel Coleman Sr, James Daniel, Williams Daniel, Farrer, Thomas Guttery, Benjamin Harrison, James Holloway Sr, James Holloway Jr, John Holloway Sr, William Holloway, Robert Hudgens, Thomas Hughes, Robert Lowry, Jonas Meador, John Moore, Jacob Mosby, Richard Murray, Alexander Speirs, Nicholas Speirs, Thomas Tabb, Thomas Tilman, Alexander Trent, Ambrose Wood, Joseph Woodson [69]

Precinct #5
Boundaries: All the lands between Tearwallet Creek and Great Guinea Creek up to the Main Road [53]

Processioners: Daniel Coleman Jr, William Womack, William Arnold, John Woodson
Landowners: Isaac Allen, James Allen, Henry Arnold, William Arnold, William Basham Sr, William Basham Jr, David Bradley, Charles Bostick, John Chafin, Daniel Coleman Jr, William Chumley, William Davis, Henry Harman, Thomas Harris, James Holland, Thomas Huckaby, Robert Lowry, Henry Macon, Josiah Payne, Paul Pigg, Martin Slaughter, John Smith, James Terry, William Womack, John Woodson [63]

Precinct #6
Boundaries: All the lands between the Main Road, [Appomattox] River, Great Guinea Creek, including William Macon's upper lines, down Angola Creek [53]
Processioners: [smudged] Allen, Joshua Doss, Ambrose Ranson, William Angel

Precinct #7
Boundaries: All the lands above William Macon's upper line and Angola Creek between Appomattox River and Great Guinea Creek [54]
Processioners: Thomas Cock, Edward Davidson, Thomas Williams, Edward McGehee, Nehemiah Glenn, John Cooke

Precinct #8
Boundaries: All the lands between the Main Road, Tearwallet Creek and Guinea Road [54]
Processioners: John Bostick, Humphrey Keeble, William Watson

Precinct #9
Boundaries: All the lands below Guinea Road between the [Appomattox] River and the Main Road, down the Road that leads to Clements' Mill [54]
Processioners: Richard Parker, Daniel Terry, George Cox

Precinct #10
Boundaries: All the lands from the county line, up Appomattox River to Genito Bridge, down Genito Road to the county line [54]
Processioners: William Marshall, Richard Mosley, William Mosley
Return: "quiet and peaceable procession is agreed on by all parties within our bounds except George Williamson and George Todd deceased" [67]

Precinct #11
Boundaries: All the lands from Genito Road up the Church Road to Buckingham Road, down Buckingham Road to the county line, along the county line to Genito Road, up the Genito Road to the Church Road [54]

Processioners: John Watkins, Joseph Baugh, Abraham Baugh
Return: "we have viewed and new marked the several lines" [65]

Precinct #12
Boundaries: All the land from Genito Bridge up the [Appomattox] River to Fighting Creek, up
              lower Fighting Creek to Buckingham Road at Worley's Church, down the Church
              Road to Genito Road, up Genito Road to the bridge [54]
Processioners: Henry Clay, William Clay, George Williamson
Landowners: Henry Clay, William Clay, John Eggleston, Thomas Hall, John Moseley, Thomas
              Moseley, Richard Randolph, William Randolph, John Stewart, Timson, George
              Williamson [64]

Precinct #13
Boundaries: All the lands from the [Worley's] Church, up Buckingham Road to Col. Randolphs,
              down the Mill Creek to the fork, up the lower fork to the Church [55]
Processioners: John Mossom, Thomas Hall, John Mosley
Landowners: John Baskerville, Thomas Bassett, John Blackburn, Henry Clay, Richard Clay,
              Charles Davis, James Davis, John Hales deceased, Thomas Hall, Samuel Hatcher,
              Richard Ligon, William Maxey, Edward Moseley, John Moseley, John Mossom,
              Richard Povall, Richard Randolph deceased, William Randolph, John Radford [65]

Precinct #14
Boundaries: All the land from the mouth of Fighting Creek up the [Appomattox] River to
              Childreys, down the said Road to Col. Randolph, down the Mill Creek to the River
              [55]
Processioners: Benjamin Childers, William Bailey, Henry Brazeal

Precinct #15
Boundaries: All the lands between the Appomattox River, Clements Mill Path, Buckingham
              Road, and the road from Benjamin Childres to Lyles Ford [55]
Processioners: William Stone, Joseph Woodson, Stephen Cox, Booker Smith

Precinct #16
Boundaries: All the lands between Deep Creek, James River, Muddy Creek, and River Road [55]
Processioners: Robert Hughes Jr, Micajah Mosby, Abraham Baker
Landowners: John Alexander, Thomas Bedford, George Going, ? Hughes, ? Mosby, ? Moss,
              Pleasants, Mr. Randolph, Edward Scruggs, John Stevenson, William Stratton,
              Thomas Tucker, Abraham Womack [68]

Precinct #17
Boundaries: All the lands between Muddy Creek, James River, Willis Creek, and River Road [55]
Processioners: Robert Carter Jr, John Carter, Henry Dillion

Precinct #18
Boundaries: All the lands between Muddy Creek, the River Road, Deep Creek, Middle Road, and Samuel Scott's Road to Muddy Creek [55]
Processioners: William Moss Jr, William Stratton, Abraham Womack
Landowners: Thomas Bedford, Bowler Cocke, Nicholas Davies, Robert Hughes, Absalom Jordan, Jacob Mosby, Joseph Mosby, Micajah Mosby, Alexander Moss, Thomas Moss, William Moss, John Pleasants, Henry Stratton, William Stratton, Edward Tabb, Noel Waddell, Abraham Womack [66]

Precinct #19
Boundaries: All the lands between Muddy Creek, the River Road, the Path from the Widow Dillion by Thomas Potter and John Salmon to Ham Chapel and the Chapel Road [55]
Processioners: Ralph Flipping, William Terrell, Orlando Hughes
Return: "we have processioned the lands and marked the lines except John Salmon, Rachel Farris, Nicholas Davies, Benjamin Harrison, John Blevins, John Rowland, Michael Rowland, Benjamin Dumas, Stephen Hughes" [67]

Precinct #20
Boundaries: All the land between the Widow Dillion's Path by Thomas Potter and John Salmons to Ham Chapel, Hugh Pruit's Path from the Chapel to Barnard's Road, and the Road to Willis Creek and the New Road, [Willis River] [56]
Processioners: James Cunningham Jr, Jonathan Cunningham, Samuel Bridgewater

Precinct #21
Boundaries: All the lands between Willis Creek, Randolphs Creek, the county line, and the new road [56]
Processioners: John Reynolds, Job Thomas, Thomas Christian

Precinct #22
Boundaries: All the lands between Willis Creek, the James River, the county line, and the new road [56]
Processioners: Samuel Taylor, Phineas Glover, Edward Daniel

Precinct #23

Boundaries: All the lands between Muddy Creek, Barnard's Road, Hugh Pruit's Path, and the Chapel Road [56]

Processioners: John Merryman, Thomas Walton, Thomas Merryman

Precinct #24

Boundaries: All the lands between Deep Creek, Mrs. Mayo's Chair Road, and the Middle Road [56]

Processioners: George Chambers, Jacob Mosby, Littleberry Mosby

Precinct #25

Boundaries: All the lands between Deep Creek, the Middle Road, Mr. Sally's Path, Buckingham Road, up Buckingham Road to Harris' Path, along Harris' Path to the beginning [56]

Processioners: Richard Cardwell, John Cardwell, Samuel Phelps

Landowners: "we have marked the within mentioned bounds laving one line between Mrs. Anne Mayo and Francis Steger" [62]

Precinct #26

Boundaries: All the lands between Willis Creek, Buckingham Road, the county line, and Randolph Creek [56]

Processioners: Benjamin Harrison, Thomas Tabb, John Bradley

Precinct #27

Boundaries: All the lands between Barnard's Road, Horn Quarter Road, [Harrison's Road], and Willis Creek [57]

Processioners: John Hollaway, William Hollaway, John Minter

Precinct #28

Boundaries: All the land between Deep Creek, the James River, the Chapel Road, and the Road from Michaux to Spears, along the Path from Howard's Quarter to Solomon's Creek, down the same to the River [57]

Processioners: John Taylor, William Taylor, Joel Chandler, John Hyde Sanders, Daniel Johnson, William Spears

Return: "we have renewed and marked the within mentioned bounds of land" [66]

Precinct #29

Boundaries: All the land from the James River, up the Road from Jacob Michaux's Ferry to Paul Michaux, the Court House Road to Solomon's Creek [57]

Processioners: Paul Michaux, Daniel Coleman, Frederick Cox

Precinct #30
Boundaries: All the land between Michaux Ferry, [James River,] and Fine Creek, [River Road]
                 up the Road to Paul Michaux [57]
Processioners: Robert Hughes, Stephen Hughes, John Railey
Return: "we have caused all the lines to be new marked except part of one line between John
                 Pleasants and Susannah Gasper" [67]

Precinct #31
Boundaries: All the lands between Fine Creek, the Middle Road to Paul Michaux & William
                 Spiers, and Fine Creek at the Three Bridges [57]
Processioners: Francis Epperson, Robert Bagby, Daniel Wilmore

Precinct #32
Boundaries: All the lands between Fine Creek, Buckingham Road, the James River, and Jones
                 Creek [57]
Processioners: John Cannafax, Nathaniel Maxey, Bennett Goode

Precinct #33
Boundaries: All the lands between Jones Creek, Buckingham Road, and the French Line [57]
Processioners: John Radford, William Maxey, Richard Epperson

Precinct #34
Boundaries: All the lands between Col. Randolph, the Church Road, the Middle Road and
                 Buckingham Road and the Negroes Arm Road [error] to Mrs. Mayo's Road [58]
Processioners: James Davis, James Ligon, Richard Ligon

Precinct #35
Boundaries: All the lands between the Middle Road, Randolph, the Church Road, Buckingham
                 Road & Mr. Sally (or the Ridge) Path [58]
Processioners: Sanburn Woodson, George Cardwell, George Owen
Landowners: "we have processioned and renewed all of the lines within our precincts except a
                 piece of Col. William Randolph's" [64]

A family coach leaving a Southern ordinary

Illustration from *Colonial Living*
by Edwin Tunis

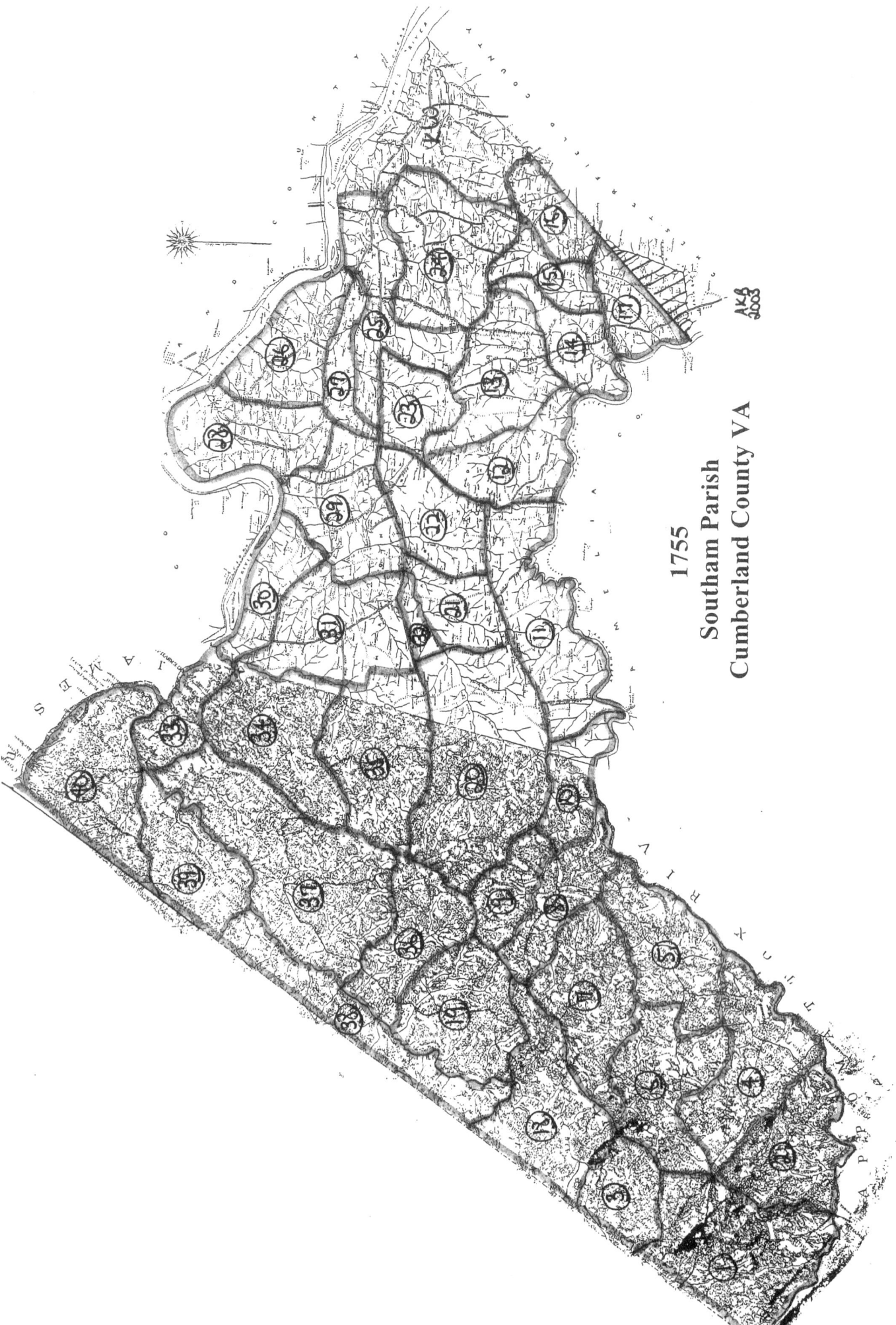

1755
Southam Parish
Cumberland County VA

1755 Cumberland County

This the third processioning conducted for Southam Parish. The orders are dated August 11, 1755, pages [77-83], and the returns April 19, 1756, pages [86-103]. Of the 40 precincts, 21 reported full returns for a return rate of 54%. Some of these orders are incomplete or missing parts. Uncertain boundaries between #5 and #6, between #19 and #36.

Precinct #1
Boundaries: Between Randolphs Road, Brooks Road, the County Line, [Appomattox River] [77]
Processioners: Charles Anderson, John Woodson, Thomas Williams, George Right
Landowners: only failures returned: Thomas Bassett, Henry Bell, Thomas Hodges deceased, Isham Richardson, Alexander Trent [87]

Precinct #2
Boundaries: Between Green Creek, Appomattox River, and Randolph's Road [77]
Processioners: James Anderson, James Allen, Thomas Cocke, Charles Cotterell
Landowners: no return

Precinct #3
Boundaries: Between Brooks Road, the County Line, Bollings Road, and the Main Road [78]
Processioners: Thomas Merryman, John Retterford Sr, Higginson Barksdale
Landowners: no return

Precinct #4
Boundaries: Between Angola Creek, Appomattox River, Green Creek, and Randolph Road [78]
Processioners: John Cook, Phillip Holcomb, Warren Walker, John Nelson
Landowners: William Angela, William Bailey, James Brown, John Brown, Zachariah Brown, Thomas Cocke, John Cook, Valentine Corley, David Davison, William Davison, Richard Epperson, Ambrose Hammon, John Hammon Sr, John Mayo, John Nelson, Matthew Nelson, Col. Peter Randolph, Ambrose Ranson, Ambrose Ranson Jr, Jonas Reynolds, Robert Tenham, James Townes, Watkins, James Walker, Joel Walker, Warren Walker, Richard Ward, George Wright, John Wright [89]

Precinct #5
Boundaries: Between Great Guinea Creek, Appomattox River, Angola Creek, and Col. William Macon's upper Lines [78]
Processioners: Isaac Allen, Joshua Doss, James Daniel, Francis Epperson
Landowners: no return

Precinct #6
Boundaries: Beginning at Col. William Macon's upper Line to Angola [Creek], up Angola to
               Randolph's Road, down Randolph's Road to Glenn's Path, on the same to Great
               Guinea, down the same to the beginning [78]
Processioners: Edward McGehee, Charles Lee, Nehemiah Glenn
Landowners: Thomas Arnold, William Angela, William Basham, Christopher Chafin, John Brown
               Cooper, Francis Epperson, Gideon Glenn, James Glenn, Charles Lee, Col. Macon,
               ? Mayo, Edward McGehee, Thomas Merryman, [?] Pleasant, ? Scott [88]

Precinct #7
Boundaries: Between Tearwallet Run, Great Guinea Creek, and the Main Road [78]
Processioners: Henry Macon, William Womack, Daniel Coleman Jr
Landowners: James Allen Sr, William Arnold, Richard Bandy, William Basham Sr, John Chafin,
               Daniel Coleman Jr, Williams Daniel, Dr. Thomas Forster, James Holland, Henry
               Macon, Edward McGehee, William Womack [92]

Precinct #8
Boundaries: Between Little Guinea Creek, Appomattox River, Great Guinea, Tearwallet Run, and
               the Main Road [78]
Processioners: John Bostick, Richard Weatherford, Henry Davenport, Henry Harman
Landowners: William Arnold, John Boles, Ackillis Bowker, Daniel Coleman, Richard Daniel,
               James Davenport, Thomas Davenport Sr, Thomas Davenport Jr, John Farmer,
               William Hambleton, Henry Harman, orphan of Hodges, John Hubbard, Mary
               Jenkins, orphan of Jenkins, Harrison Jones, John Jones, Gideon Marr, Samuel
               Meredith, Martin Slaughter, John Smith, John Taylor, William Trigg, Christopher
               Watson, William Watson, Richard Weatherford, William Womack [90]

Precinct #9
Boundaries: Between Little Guinea Creek, the Main Road, and Guinea Road [79]
Processioners: Humphrey Keeble, William Hambleton, William Watson
Landowners: Francis Allen, Julius Allen, William Arnold, John Burton, Christopher Chalton,
               James Daniel, Thomas Davenport Sr, John Farmer, ? Freeman, William Hambleton,
               Adolphus Hendricks, John Hubbard, Joseph Jenkins, Mary Jenkins, Harrison Jones,
               John Jones, Humphrey Keeble, Gideon Marr, Susannah Martin, William Martin,
               Samuel Meredith, James Patterson, Thomas Riddle, Richard Sharp, William Watson,
               Thomas Whitton, John Woodson [88]

Precinct #10
Boundaries: Between Little Guinea Creek, Guinea Road, Appomattox River, Buckingham Road,
               and the Road to Clements' Mill [79]

Processioners: Robert Thomson, Richard Parker, Lawrence Smith
Landowners: William Allen, Samuel Burton, Citt [Christopher] Chalton, George Cox, Hall Cox, Richard Daniel, ? Freeman, John Blan Horton, Hatcher, Isaac Hughes, Murray, Richard Parker, Richard Parker Jr, William Parker, Smith, Robert Thomson, Yarborough [100]

Precinct #11
Boundaries: Between Appomattox River, Lyles Road, Buckingham Road, and the road to Clements' Mill [79]
Processioners: Ackillis Bowker, Joseph Woodson, Bowker Smith, Nathaniel Ford
Landowners: "marked and renewed every line" but no names returned [97]

Precinct #12
Boundaries: Between Appomattox River, Fighting Creek, Buckingham Road, and Lyles' Road [79]
Processioners: Richard Povall, Benjamin Childrey, William Bailey
Landowners: William Bailey, Henry Brazeal, James Cock, William Elam, Nicholas Giles, William Hudspeth, Nathaniel Maxey, William Randolph, William Smith, Phillip Thomas, Richard Williamson [104]

Precinct #13
Boundaries: Between the fork of Fighting Creek, up Randolph's Mill Creek to Buckingham Road, down the Road to the [South] Church, down the Creek to the fork [79]
Processioners: John Moseley, Edward Moseley, Henry Clay
Landowners: "all done in peace and quietness" but no names returned [93]

Precinct #14
Boundaries: Between Genito Road, the Church Road, Fighting Creek, and Appomattox River
Processioners: Francis Marshall, Thomas Locket, Joel Locket [79]
Landowners: Larkin Chew, Henry Clay, William Clay, Thomas Hamblet, John Mosley, Thomas Mosley, Bret Randolph, William Randolph, John Stort, Timson [101]

Precinct #15
Boundaries: Between the New Road, Buckingham Road, the Church Road, and Genito Road [79]
Processioners: Edward Watkins, Isham Akins, Abraham Baugh
Landowners: "all the lines" marked and viewed, no names returned [94]

Precinct #16

Boundaries: Between Buckingham Road, the New Road, Genito Road, and the County Line

Processioners: Joseph Baugh, Israel Winfrey, John Watkins

Landowners: "we have viewed and new marked all the lines" but no names returned [101]

Precinct #17

Boundaries: Between the County Line, Appomattox River, and Genito Road [80]

Processioners: George Hancock, Richard Mosley, William Mosley

Landowners: Christopher Bass, Lodowick Elam, Creed Haskins, George Hancock, Gideon Lockett, Joel Lockett, Francis Marshall, William Marshall, Arthur Mosley, Benjamin Mosley, Richard Mosley, William Mosley, John Northcutt, Mark Taylor, Timson, Todd, Tomson, Edward Watkins [99]

Precinct #18

Boundaries: Between Bollings Road, Buckingham Road, the Main Road, and the County line [80]

Processioners: Williams Daniel, William Mills, William Trigg

Landowners: James Brown, John Bullock, Daniel Coleman, Williams Daniel, Warham Easley, Ralph Flipping, Henry Garrett, Thomas Guttery, John Harrelson, Adolphus Hendricks, Thomas Johns, John Kendall, Anthony Levillion deceased, John Martin, William Mills, Robert Kent, Alexander Speirs, Thomas Tabb, Tarewallet Church, Zachariah Terry, Alexander Trent, William Trigg, James Wilkins [89]

Precinct #19

Boundaries: Between Buckingham Road, the County line [error, should be Willis River], Harrison's Road, and the Road from Murrays to John Burtons [80]

Processioners: Samuel Allen, Alexander Trent, Thomas Guttery

Landowners: no return

Precinct #20

Boundaries: Between Buckingham Road, the Road from John Burtons to Murrays, the Courthouse Road, and Mayo's Old Mill Path to Benjamin Harris' [80]

Processioners: John Hobson, William Hobson, Field Robertson, George Winneford

Landowners: Samuel Allen, James Anderson, Abraham Bailey, John Bolton, John Bradley, John Burton, Daniel Coleman Sr, Thomas Coleman, Williams Daniel, Joseph Farrar, Samuel Gladoe, Thomas Guttery, Benjamin Harrison, William Hix Sr, Thomas Holland, William Holland, James Holloway, James Holloway Jr, John Holloway Sr, Robert Hudgens, Samuel Jones, Robert Lowery, Jonas Meadors Sr, Samuel Milton, Robert Moore, Richard Murray, Randolph Rickerson, William Rowland, Alexander Speirs, Nicholas Speirs, Thomas Tabb, David Thomson, Thomas Tilman, Alexander Trent, Ambrose Wood, Joseph Woodson [98]

Precinct #21

Boundaries: Between the Middle Road, Mr. Salley's Path, Buckingham Road, Mr. Harris' Path to Mayo Old Mill and Deep Creek [80]

Processioners: Poindexter Mosby, John Scruggs, John Hughes

Landowners: "we have processioned all the lands except Jacob Woodson," no other names returned [101]

Precinct #22

Boundaries: Between the Middle Road, Randolph's Church Road, Buckingham Road, and Mr. Salley's Path [80]

Processioners: Sanburn Woodson, George Owen, George Cardwell, Francis McCraw

Landowners: Joseph Atkins, Widow Barnes, Collier Basdale, George Cardwell, Daniel Carter, Benjamin Childrey, William Hudspeth, Marmaduke Hix, John Howlett, Daniel Mayo, Francis McCraw, John Netherland, Samuel Olsen, ? Osburn, George Owen, John Phelps, John Pleasants, William Randolph, Abraham Salley, John Hyde Saunders, William Smith, Thomas Walker, Charity Woodson, Owen Woodson, Sanburn Woodson deceased [96]

Precinct #23

Boundaries: Between the Middle Road, Randolph's Church Road, Buckingham Road, and the Road from the Negroes Arm to Mrs. Mayo's [81]

Processioners: James Davis, Richard Ligon, James Ligon

Landowners: no return

Precinct #24

Boundaries: Between Jones Creek, the French lines, and Buckingham Road [81]

Processioners: John Radford, William Maxey, Joseph Bondurant

Landowners: "all lines in peace" with no names returned [94]

Precinct #25

Boundaries: Between Jones Creek, [King William Parish line,] James River, Fine Creek, [Middle Road, Negros Arms Road], and Buckingham Road [81]

Processioners: Bennet Goode, Nathaniel Maxey, Edward Parrott

Landowners: no return

Precinct #26
Boundaries: Between Michaux Ferry Road, James River, Fine Creek, and the road to Paul
               Michaux [81]
Processioners: John Railey, Joseph Hughes, Daniel Wilmore
Landowners: no return

Precinct #27
Boundaries: Between Fine Creek, the Middle [error, should be River] Road to Paul Michaux,
               from Michaux to William Speirs and Fine Creek at the Three Bridges [81]
Processioners: Robert Bagby, Henry Bagby, William Cox
Landowners: "marked all the lines" including Mrs. Mayo, Paul Michaux, Speirs, Col. Stoner [96]

Precinct #28
Boundaries: Between James River, the Ferry Road to Paul Michaux, the Courthouse [River] Road
               to Solomon's Creek [81]
Processioners: Paul Michaux, John Franklin, Robert Chandler
Landowners: "processioned and marked all the lines" but no names returned [96]

Precinct #29
Boundaries: Between Deep Creek, [Middle Road], the Church Road, the road from Speirs to
               Michaux, [River Road], Solomons Creek, and James River [81]
Processioners: John Taylor, William Taylor, John Hyde Sanders, Daniel Johnson, William Speirs,
               Edmond Toney
Landowners: Col. Bedford, James Crafford, David Chandler, Mrs. Chandler, Timothy Chandler,
               Philip Cockaham, the Glebe, ? Howard, Daniel Johnson, ? Low, Daniel Mayo, John
               Meanley, Jacob Mosby, ? Randolph, Mrs. Randolph, Abraham Salley, John Hyde
               Saunders, Edward Scruggs, Thomas Scruggs, William Spiers, Bartholomew Stovall,
               James Taylor, John Taylor, Edmond Toney, Walton [95]

Precinct #30
Boundaries: Between Deep Creek, James River, Muddy Creek, and the River Road [82]
Processioners: Robert Hughes, Micajah Mosby, Joseph Mosby
Landowners: Alexander, Bedford, William Carr, Hughes, Mosby, Thomas Moss, Pleasants, Mrs.
               Randolph, Edward Scruggs, John Stephenson, Stratton, Womack [93]

Precinct #31
Boundaries: Between Muddy Creek, the River Road, Deep Creek, and the Middle Road [82]
Processioners: Abraham Womack, William Stratton, William Moss
Landowners: Col. Bedford, Bowler Cocke, Nicholas Davies, Charles Finch, Robert Hughes,

Micajah Mosby, Jacob Mosby, Alexander Moss, James Moss, Thomas Moss, William Moss, John Pleasant, Jane Randolph, Samuel Scott, Nicholas Spiers, Henry Stratton, William Stratton, Edward Tabb, Noel Waddell, Abraham Womack, Richard Womack [94]

Precinct #32
Boundaries: Between Deep Creek, Mrs. Mayo's Chair Road, and the Middle Road [82]
Processioners: George Chambers, Littleberry Mosby, Jacob Mosby
Landowners: Julius Allen, William Battersby, Charles Bradshaw, Field Bradshaw, John Bradshaw, Josiah Bradshaw, William Bradshaw, John Brumskil, John Burton, William Clark, Anthony Colquitt, Nicholas Cox, George Evans, Nathaniel Ford, Holman Freeman, Joseph Fuqua, Frederick Hatcher, Henry Hatcher, Adolphus Hendricks, William Holloway, John Hobson, William Hobson, John Hubbard, William Hutson, Samuel Jones, Humphrey Keeble, Stephen Mallet, William Matthis, John Mattox, John Mayo, Jonas Meador, Richard Murray, Samuel Nichols, Gideon Patterson, John Pleasants, Christopher Robertson, Edward Robertson, John Robertson, Francis George Steger, Thomas Tabb, Robert Thomson, John Wayles, David Winneford, George Winneford [103]

Precinct #33
Boundaries: Between Muddy Creek, James River, Willis Creek, and River Road [82]
Processioners: Robert Carter Jr, Henry Dillon, John Carter
Landowners: no return

Precinct #34
Boundaries: Between Muddy Creek, the River Road, the Path from the Widow Dillon by Thomas Potter and John Salmon to Ham Chapel, and the Chapel Road [82]
Processioners: Ralph Flipping, William Terrell, Orlando Hughes
Landowners: no return

Precinct #35
Boundaries: Between Muddy Creek, Barnard's Road, Hugh Prewit's Path, and the Chapel Road [82]
Processioners: John Merryman, Thomas Walton, Richard Murray
Landowners: "we processioned all the lands" but no names returned [97]

Precinct #36
Boundaries: Between Barnard's Road, Horn Quarter Road, [Buckingham Road], and Willis Creek [83]

Processioners: William Holland, John Minter, Christopher Dickens
Landowners: James Anderson, James Brown, Samuel Browne, Joseph Butler, Andrew Edwards, William Holland, James Holloway Sr, John Holloway, William Holloway, John Minter, Job Thomas [93]

Precinct #37
Boundaries: Between the Widow Dillon's Path by Thomas Potter and John Salmon to Ham Chapel, Hugh Prewit's Path to Barnard's Road, the said Road to Willis Creek, the said Creek and the River Road [83]
Processioners: James Cunningham, Jonathan Cunningham, Samuel Bridgewater
Landowners: Francis Amoss, John Armstead, Samuel Atkins, William Bolling, William Bond, Samuel Bridgewater, Samuel Brown, John Carter, George Carrington, Thomas Christian, William Clark, Edward Clements, John Cox, Alexander Cunningham, James Cunningham, Jonathan Cunningham, Christopher Dickens, Henry Dillon, William Dillon, Andrew Edwards, John Fleming, Carter Harrison, John Hill, John McGuire, Jonas Meador, Jacob Michaux, Joseph Price, John Robertson, John Salmon, Robert Smith, John Tatum, Job Thomas [97]

Precinct #38
Boundaries: Between Willis Creek, Buckingham Road, the County line, and Randolph's Creek [83]
Processioners: Benjamin Harrison, Thomas Tabb, Benjamin Wilson
Landowners: John Bartee, Archibald Cary, Robert Burton, Watt Daniel, Joseph Farrar, Benjamin Harrison, John Jude, Leonard Keeling, David McCormack, Drury Scruggs, Alexander Spiers, Thomas Tabb, Job Thomas, David Thomson, Alexander Trent, Field Trent, Benjamin Wilson [92]

Precinct #39
Boundaries: Between Willis Creek, Randolph's Creek, the county line, and River Road [83]
Processioners: Job Thomas, John Reynolds, Thomas Christian
Landowners: Benjamin Cannon, George Carrington, James Cunningham, William Evans, Phineas Glover, Edward Hambleton, Maurice Langhorn, Valentine Martin, Joseph Price, David Reynolds, Job Thomas, David Thomson [101]

Precinct #40
Boundaries: Between Willis Creek, James River, the county Line, and River Road [83]
Processioners: Samuel Taylor, Phineas Glover, Benjamin Cannon
Landowners: John Burnett, Benjamin Cannon, George Carrington, Robert Carter, Robert Carter Jr, Elizabeth Hooper, Daniel Jones, Phillip Mayo, James Nevil deceased, David Prior, Michael Rowland, Reuben Skelton, Samuel Taylor [102]

August 11th 1755

Ordered That Joseph Baugh Israel Winfrey and John Watkins on the 10th Day of November Next Begin and Procession all the Lands and Renew and mark the several Lines Between Buckingame Road the New Road Peneto Road and the County Line and make their Return according to Law ————

Ordered That George Hancock, Richard Moseley and William Moseley on the 10th Day of November next Begin and Procession all the Lands and Renew and Mark the several Lines Between the County Line Appamattox River and Peneto Road and make their Return according to Law ————

Ordered That Williams Daniel William Mills and William Trigg on the 10th Day of November next Begin and Procession all the Lands and Renew And mark the several lines Between Bollings Road Buckingame Road The main Road and the County line and make their Return according to Law ————

Ordered That Samuell allen, Alexander Trent and Thomas Puttery on the 10th Day Of November next Begin and Procession all the Lands and Renew and mark The several lines Between Buckingame Road the County line Harrisons Road And the Road from Murrays to John Burtons And make their Return according to Law ————

Ordered That John Hopson William Hopson Field Robertson and George Winneford on the 10th Day of November Next Begin and Procession all the Lands and Renew And mark the several lines Between Buckingame Road the Road from John Burton To murrays the Courthouse Road and mayos old mill Path to Benjamin Harris's And make their Return according to Law ————

Ordered That Poindexter Mosby John Scriggs and John Hughes on the 10th Day of November Next Begin and Procession all the Lands and Renew and mark the several lines Between the middle Road mr Talleys Path Buckingame Road mr Harris's Path to mayo old mill and Deep Creek and make their Return according to Law ————

Ordered That Tarlton Woodson George Owen George Cardwell and Frances Macraw on the 10th Day of November next Begin and Procession all the Lands and Renew and mark the several Lines Between the middle Road Randolphs Church Road Buckingame Road and mr Talleys Path And make their Return according to Law ————

Page 80 from the Vestry Book with processioning orders dated August 11 1755

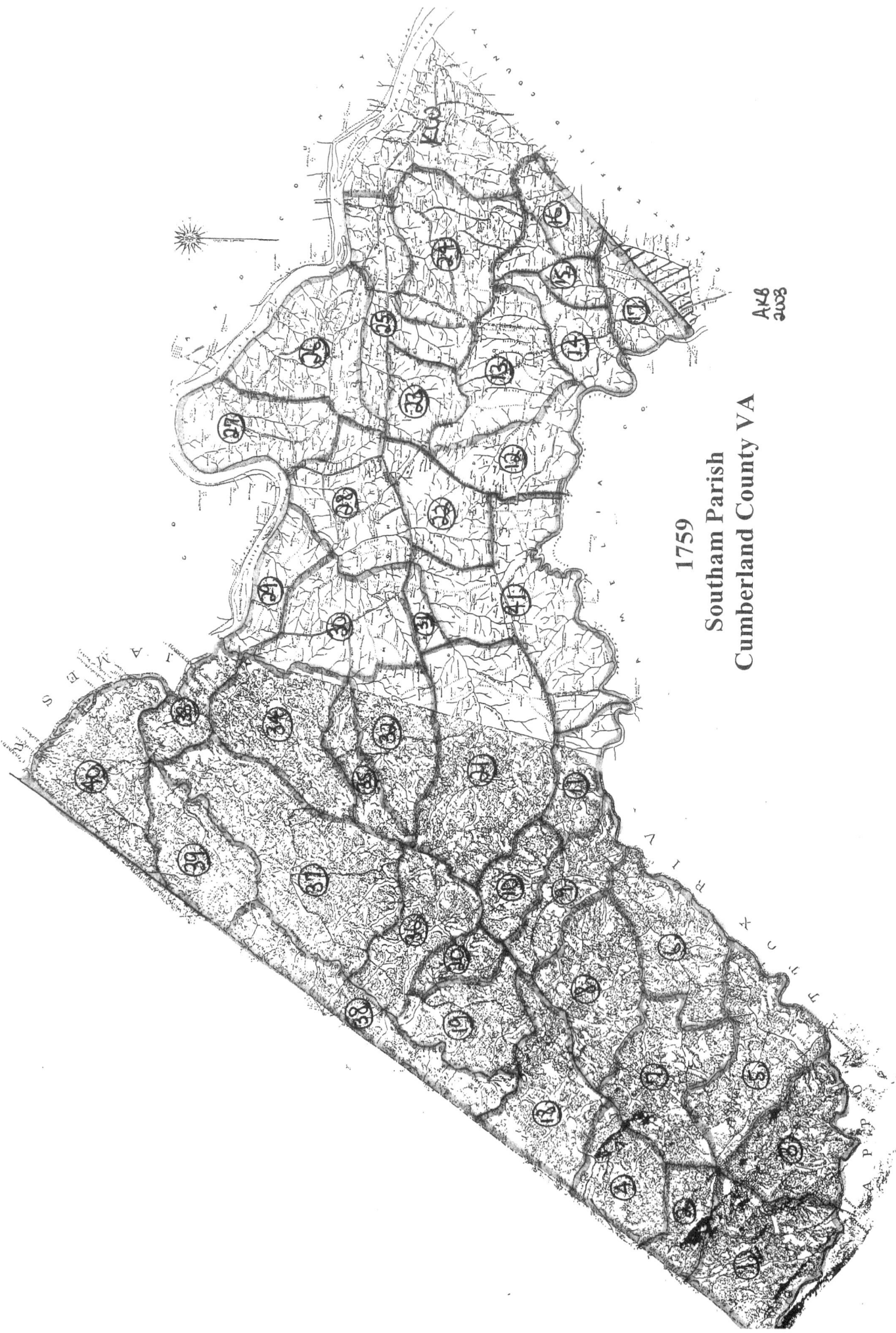

1759
Southam Parish
Cumberland County VA

1759 Cumberland County

This the fourth processioning conducted for Southam Parish. The orders are dated August 11, 1759, pages [112-117] and the returns August 22, 1760, pages [121-132]. Of the 41 precincts, only 14 reported full returns for a return rate of 34%. Uncertain boundaries between # 6 and #7, and between #32 and #35.

Precinct #1
Boundaries: Between Randolph's Road, Clover Forrest Road, and the county line, [Appomattox River] [112]
Processioners: Charles Anderson, John Woodson, Saymore Scott
Landowners: Charles Anderson, James Anderson, Robert Hall, William Hall, Leander Hughes, Powell Hughes, Ryland Randolph, Isham Richerson, Saymore Scott, Charles Williams, Roger Williams, John Woodson, George Wright [123]

Precinct #2
Boundaries: Between Randolph's Road, Clover Forrest Road, the county line, and Brooks Road [112]
Processioners: George Wright, Thomas Williams, John Wright, Charles Lee
Landowners: Henry Bell, Archibald Cary, John Gannaway, Robert Johns, Ryland Randolph, Isham Richerson, Alexander Trent, Peterfield Trent, Charles Williams, Thomas Williams, George Wright [123]

Precinct #3
Boundaries: Between Appomattox River, Green Creek, and Randolph's Road [112]
Processioners: Matthias Williams, John Chambers, Charles Cotterel, Aaron Butler
Landowners: no return

Precinct #4
Boundaries: Between Brooks Road and county line, Bollings [road] and the Main Road [112]
Processioners: Higginson Barksdale, Julius Davenport, John Retterford Sr, Thomas Jeffries
Landowners: no return

Precinct #5
Boundaries: Between Angola Creek, Appomattox River, Green Creek, and Randolph's Road [112]
Processioners: John Cook, James Brown, Warren Walker, William Bailey
Landowners: no return

Precinct #6
Boundaries: Between Great Guinea Creek, Appomattox River, Angola Creek, and Col. William
               Macon's upper Lines [112]
Processioners: Culvarine Ford, Dudley Roundtree, Francis Epperson
Landowners: no return

Precinct #7
Boundaries: Beginning at Col. William Macon's upper lines, to Angola Creek, up the creek to
               Randolph's Road, down the road to Glenn's Path, on the same to Great Guinea
               Creek, down the same to the beginning [113]
Processioners: Edward McGehee, Nathan Glenn, William Anglea Jr
Landowners: no return

Precinct #8
Boundaries: Between Tearwallet Run, Great Guinea Creek, [Glenn's Path], and the Main Road
               [113]
Processioners: Henry Macon, William Womack, Daniel Coleman Jr, John Noel
Landowners: "we gave our attendance, but no one appeared" [122]

Precinct #9
Boundaries: Between Little Guinea Creek, Appomattox River, Great Guinea Creek, Tearwallet
               Run, and the Ridge Road [113]
Processioners: Henry Davenport, Henry Harman, Richard Weatherford, Richard Daniel
Landowners: William Arnold, John Boles, John Bostick, Richard Daniel, Henry Davenport, James
               Davenport, Joseph Davenport, Philemon Davenport, Stephen Davenport, Thomas
               Davenport Jr, William Davenport, Henry Farmer, John Farmer, Henry Harman,
               William Hambleton, Orphan Hodges, James Hubbard, Joseph Hubbard, Joseph
               Jenkins, Mary Jenkins, Orphans Jenkins, Harrison Jones, John Jones, Maurice
               Langhorne, Samuel Meredith, Benjamin Sims, John Smith, George Slaughter,
               Christopher Watson, William Watson, Richard Weatherford, William Womack
               [124,125]

Precinct #10
Boundaries: Between Little Guinea Creek, Buckingham Road, and Guinea Road [113]
Processioners: William Watson, Henry Farmer, John Jonas, Francis Allen
Landowners: no return

Precinct #11
Boundaries: Between Appomattox River, Little Guinea Creek, Guinea Road, Buckingham Road, and the Road to Clements Mill [113]
Processioners: Lawrence Smith, Robert Thomson, Richard Parker, George Cox
Landowners: Francis Allen, Burton, Christopher Chalton, George Cox, Hall Cox, Henry Cox, Richard Daniel, Allen Freeman, Frederick Hatcher, Henry Hatcher, Mrs. Hughes, Thomas Merryman, Thomas Osley?, Richard Parker Sr, Widow Parker, Patteson, Pringle, Richards, Robert Scruggs, Lawrence Smith, Josiah Thompson, Benajah Thomson, John Wayles [125]

Precinct #12
Boundaries: Between Appomattox River, Fighting Creek, Buckingham Road, Lyles Road [113]
Processioners: Richard Povall, William Smith Joiner, Phillip Thomas Jr
Landowners: William Archer, William Bailey, Samuel Childress, Richard Eggleston, William Elam, John Gamon, Nicholas Giles, William Hudspeth, Osburn, Locket, Nathaniel Maxey, Richard Povall, William Randolph, William Smith, Phillip Thomas, Richard Williamson, Robert Williamson [122]

Precinct #13
Boundaries: Between from the fork of Fighting Creek, up Randolphs Mill Creek to Buckingham Road, down the road to the [South] Church, down the Creek to the fork [113]
Processioners: John Moseley, Edward Moseley, Henry Clay
Landowners: no return

Precinct #14
Boundaries: Between Genito Road, the Church Road, Fighting Creek, Appomattox River [114]
Processioners: John Cox, Thomas Locket, Joel Locket
Landowners: no return

Precinct #15
Boundaries: Between the New Road, Buckingham Road, the Church Road, and Genito Road [114]
Processioners: Edward Watkins, Isham Akin, Abraham Baugh
Landowners: Isham Akin, William Akin, Abraham Baugh, Joseph Baugh, Francis Cheatham, Joel Locket, Thomas Locket, Charles Maxey, William Maxey, Edward Mosley, John Mosley, Thomas Mosley, Walter Scott, Benjamin Watkins, Edward Watkins, John Watkins, Thomas Watkins, Thomas Wooldridge, John Worley, William Worley [126]

Precinct #16
Boundaries: Between Buckingham [Road], the New Road, Genito Road, and the county line [114]
Processioners: Israel Winfrey, Joseph Baugh, John Watkins
Landowners: no return

Precinct #17
Boundaries: Between the county line, Appomattox River, and Genito Road [114]
Processioners: George Hancock, Richard Moseley, William Moseley
Landowners: no return

Precinct #18
Boundaries: Between Bollings Road, the Main Road, Buckingham Road, and the county line [114]
Processioners: Williams Daniel, Robert Kent, William Mills, John Seay
Landowners: no return

Precinct #19
Boundaries: Between Willis River, Soakass Creek to Daniels' old houses and Buckingham old Road [114]
Processioners: Capt. Samuel Allen, Thomas Guttery, Alexander Trent
Landowners: no return

Precinct #20
Boundaries: Between Harrison's Road, the road to John Burton, Buckingham Road to Daniels' old houses and Soakass Creek [114]
Processioners: James Holloway, John Bowden, Isaac Beacham, William Rowland
Landowners: no return

Precinct #21
Boundaries: Between Buckingham Road, the road from John Burton to Murray, the Courthouse Road, and Mayo's Mill Path to Ben Harris [115]
Processioners: John Hobson, Samuel Jones, Field Robinson, William Hobson
Landowners: no return

Precinct #22
Boundaries: Between the Middle Road, Randolph's Church Road, Buckingham Road, and Mr. Salley's Path [115]

Processioners: George Owen, John Burch, John Netherland
Landowners: no return

Precinct #23
Boundaries: Between the Middle Road, Randolph's Church Road, Buckingham Road, and the road from the Negroes Arm to Mrs. Mayo [115]
Processioners: Richard Ligon, John Baskerville, William Davis
Landowners: no return

Precinct #24
Boundaries: Between Jones Creek, King William Parish Line, and Buckingham Road [115]
Processioners: Humphrey Smith, John Maxey, Thomas Ballow
Landowners: no return

Precinct #25
Boundaries: Between Jones Creek, King William Parish lines, James River, Fine Creek to the Middle Road, the Middle Road to Mrs. Mayo, Mrs. Mayo's Road to Buckingham Road [115]
Processioners: Edward Parrott, John Cannefax, George Radford
Landowners: John Archer, John Baskerville, Joseph Bondurant, John Cannefax, James Holeman, Robert Hughes, Thomas Jefferson, Richard Ligon, Walter Maxey, Joseph Mayo, John Pleasants, Thomas Prosser, George Radford, John Radford, Thomas Turpin [121]

Precinct #26
Boundaries: Between the Road from Michaux Ferry as far as Spiers Ordinary, the Middle Road to Fine Creek, down Fine Creek to James River, up the River to the Ferry [115]
Processioners: John Railey, David Seizer, Bennet Goode, Henry Hobson
Landowners: Silvater Alford, Henry Bagby, Susannah Carner, Elizabeth Cox, William Cox, John Fleming, Bennet Goode, John Hughes, Robert Hughes, Robert Hughes deceased, Richard James, Joseph Johns, Jacob Michaux, Paul Michaux, John Pleasants, John Railey, William Reynolds deceased, David Seizer (Caesor), John Spurlock, Daniel Stoner, Nicholas Wilkinson, Daniel Wilmore [130]

Precinct #27
Boundaries: Between James River, the Ferry Road to Paul Michaux, the River Road and Solomon's Creek [115]
Processioners: William Prosser, Robert Bagby, William Cox
Landowners: no return

Precinct #28
Boundaries: Between Deep Creek, the Middle Road, the road from Spiers to Paul Michaux, the River Road to Solomons Creek, Solomons Creek, James River [116]
Processioners: Bartholomew Stovall Jr, Edmond Toney, David Chandler, James Taylor (son of John Taylor deceased)
Landowners: no return

Precinct #29
Boundaries: Between Deep Creek, James River, Muddy Creek, and the River Road [116]
Processioners: Micajah Mosby, Charles Finch, John Stephenson
Landowners: James Barnes, Thomas Bedford, Charles Edwards, Charles Finch, Robert Hughes, Edward Morgan, Micajah Mosby, John Pleasant, Richard Perkins, Jane Randolph, John Scott, John Stevenson, William Stratton, Thomas Tucker, Abraham Womack [128]

Precinct #30
Boundaries: Between Muddy Creek as high as Scott's Mill, Pattesons Road to the Middle Road, the Middle Road to Deep Creek, and the River Road [116]
Processioners: James Moss, Edward Tabb, Henry Stratton
Landowners: James Aiken, Benjamin Bedford, Bowler Cocke, Nicholas Davies, Charles Finch, William Holland, Robert Hughes, Richard Ligon, Jesse Miller, Edward Morgan, Benjamin Mosby, Jacob Mosby, Micajah Mosby, Alexander Moss, James Moss, John Moss, John Pleasants, Thomas Randolph, Charles Scott, Nicholas Speirs, Francis Steger, Henry Stratton, Thomas Stratton, William Stratton, Edward Tabb, Thomas Tucker, William Tucker, Noel Waddell, Abraham Womack [129]

Precinct #31
Boundaries: Between Deep Creek, Mrs. Mayo's Chair Road and the Middle Road [116]
Processioners: Littleberry Mosby, Benjamin Mosby, Francis George Steger
Landowners: no return

Precinct #32
Boundaries: Between the Middle Road, to Murray's Ordinary, Muddy Creek to Scott's Mill, Patteson's Road to the Middle Road [116]
Processioners: Stephen Mosby, Hezekiah Mosby, George Chambers
Landowners: no return

Precinct #33

Boundaries: Between Muddy Creek, James River, Willis River, and River Road [116]

Processioners: Charles Carter, William Dillon, Henry Dillon

Landowners: no return

Precinct #34

Boundaries: Between Muddy Creek, the River Road, Carter's Ferry Road, and the Chapel Road to Scott's Mill [117]

Processioners: Orlando Hughes, William Terrell, John Creasy

Landowners: no return

Precinct #35

Boundaries: Between Muddy Creek, Barnard's Road, Carter's Ferry Road, and the Chapel Road to Muddy Creek [117]

Processioners: Ralph Flipping, Jacob Winfree, Robert Douglas

Landowners: no return

Precinct #36

Boundaries: Between Barnard's Road, Horn Quarter Road, [Harrison's Road], and Willis Creek [117]

Processioners: William Holland, Thomas Tabb, John Holland

Landowners: no return

Precinct #37

Boundaries: Between Carter's Ferry Road, Barnard's Road, Willis River, and River Road [117]

Processioners: Samuel Oslin, John Armstead, John Salmon

Landowners: no return

Precinct #38

Boundaries: Between Willis River, Buckingham Road, the county line, and Randolph's Creek [117]

Processioners: Benjamin Harrison, Benjamin Wilson, Drury Scruggs

Landowners: Capt. Allen, Archibald Cary, Joseph Farrar, John Jude, Benjamin Harrison, Leonard Keeling, Drury Scruggs, Thomas Tabb, Alexander Trent, Benjamin Wilson, Tucker Woodson [124]

Precinct #39
Boundaries: Between Willis River, Randolph's Creek, the county line, and River Road [117]
Processioners: Phineas Glover, John Reynolds, Joseph Price
Landowners: Benjamin Cannon, Jeremiah Cannon, George Carrington, Paul Carrington, Thomas
               Christian, Valentine Christian, James Cunningham, James Gilliam, Phineas Glover,
               Maurice Langhorn, Gideon Martin, Orson Martin, Valentine Martin, Joseph Price,
               David Reynolds, John Reynolds, Samuel Taylor, Job Thomas, Alexander Trent,
               Benjamin Walker, Drury Woodson [127]

Precinct #40
Boundaries: Between Willis River, James River, the county line, and River Road [117]
Processioners: Samuel Taylor, Benjamin Cannon
Landowners: Benjamin Cannon, Jeremiah Cannon, George Carrington, Thomas Field, James
               Gilliam, Phineas Glover, Phillip Mayo, John Prior, David Reynolds, Samuel Taylor,
               William Rowland [128]

Precinct #41
Boundaries: Between Deep Creek, the Middle Road to Salley's Path, to Buckingham Road, to
               Lyles' Road, to Appomattox River, to Clements Mill, on Clements Mill Road to
               Buckingham Road, down the same to Mr. Harris' Mill Path, on the same to Mayo
               Old Mill [117]
Processioners: Poindexter Mosby, Roderick Easley, Joseph Woodson, John Hughes
Landowners: no return

Old tobacco barn

Illustrations from *Colonial Living*
by Edwin Tunis

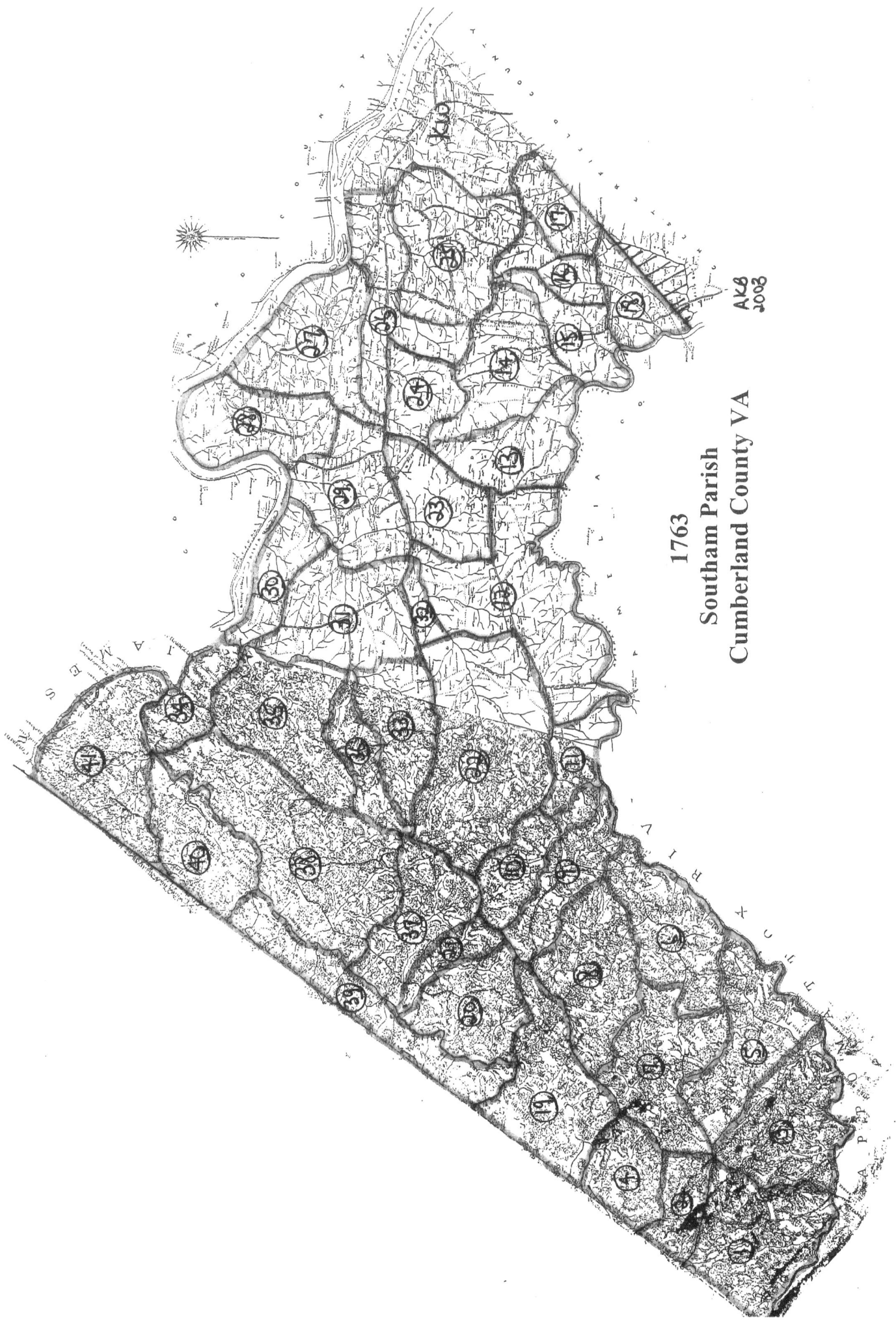

1763
Southam Parish
Cumberland County VA

1763 Cumberland County

This the fifth processioning conducted for Southam Parish. The orders are dated July 23, 1763, pages [143-147], and the returns February 27, 1765, pages [152-172]. Of the 41 precincts, 33 reported full returns for the highest return rate of 80%. Uncertain boundary between #33 and #36.

Precinct #1
Boundaries: Between Randolphs Road, the Clover Forrest Road, and the county line [143]
Processioners: Charles Anderson, Saymore Scott, James Anderson
Landowners: Charles Anderson, James Anderson, Samuel Phelps, Richard Randolph, Mary Richerson, Saymore Scott, William Shepard, Charles Williams, Roger Williams, John Woodson, Ambrose Wright, George Wright [167]

Precinct #2
Boundaries: Between Randolph's Road, the Clover Forrest Road, the county line, and Brooks Road [143]
Processioners: George Wright, Thomas Williams, Robert Johns
Landowners: Henry Bell, Thomas Davenport, John Gannaway, Robert Johns, Richard Randolph, Alexander Trent, Peterfield Trent, Charles Williams, Thomas Williams, George Wright, "not all giving their attendance" [166]

Precinct #3
Boundaries: Between Appomattox River, Green Creek, and Randolph's Road [143]
Processioners: John Raine, Joseph Michaux, John Chambers
Landowners: Anderson, Aaron Butler, John Chambers, Thomas Cocke estate, John Cook, Charles Cottrell, Fretwell, Hughes, Johnson, Moore Lumpkin, Joseph Michaux, Henry Pattillo, Peter Randolph, Richard Randolph, Ryland Randolph, Ray, Warren Walker, Matthias Williams, John Woodson, Ambrose Wright [165]

Precinct #4
Boundaries: Between Brooks Road, the county line, Bollings Road, and the Main Road [143]
Processioners: Thomas Johns, Jarrett Ellison, William Hudgens Jr
Landowners: John Archer, Joseph Calland, Archibald Cary, Julius Davenport, Thomas Davenport, Gerard Ellison, Grisham, Robert Hudgens, William Hudgens, Robert Hughes, Joseph Johns, Thomas Johns, Alexander Trent, James Watkins, James Wilkins, John Woodson [153]

Precinct #5
Boundaries: Between Angola Creek, Appomattox River, Green Creek, and Randolphs Road [143]
Processioners: Warren Walker, James Brown, John Wright, John Holeman
Landowners: James Anglea, William Anglea, William Anglea Jr, James Archdeacon, James Brown, John Brown, Zachariah Brown, Thomas Carter, John Cook, Valentine Corley, Isaac Duffy, Joseph Hammon, John Holeman, John Lee, John Mayo, John Nelson, Matt Nelson, William Owen, John Pleasants, John Raine, Peter Randolph, Flamsteed Ranson, James Reynolds, Jonas Reynolds, William Shepard, James Townes, William Walker, Richard Ward, Nat Watkins, Thomas Webb, Thomas Webb, Ambrose Wright, John Wright [162]

Precinct #6
Boundaries: Between Great Guinea Creek, Appomattox River, Angola Creek, and Col. William Macon's upper lines [143]
Processioners: Isaac Allen, Matthew Nelson, John Nelson
Landowners: "we advertised and met and for want of attendance, could not procession" [165]

Precinct #7
Boundaries: Between beginning at Col. William Macon's upper lines, Angola Creek, up the same to Randolph's Road, down the same to Glenn's Path, on the same to Great Guinea Creek, down the same to the beginning [143]
Processioners: Nathan Glenn, William Anglea Jr, Charles Lee
Landowners: William Anglea Sr, William Anglea Jr, John Brown, Joseph Calland, Christopher Chafin, Abraham Chalton, Davenport, James Dorham, Francis Epperson, Gideon Glenn, Robert Johns, Thomas Johns, Charles Lee, William Macon, Mrs. Mayo, Edward McGehee, John Pleasants, Flemsteed Ranson, Thomas Wright, and others not processioned [159]

Precinct #8
Boundaries: Between Tarwallet Run, Great Guinea Creek, as high as Glenn's Path, and the Main Road [144]
Processioners: William Womack, Daniel Coleman Jr, Daniel Allen, Mark Andrews
Landowners: "for want of attendance could not possession the land within our precinct" [168]

Precinct #9
Boundaries: Between Little Guinea Creek, Appomattox River, Great Guinea Creek, Tarwallet Run, and the Main Ridge Road [144]
Processioners: Charles Ballow, William Hambleton, William Davenport, Henry Harmon
Landowners: William Arnold, William Arnold Jr, Charles Ballow, John Boles, Joseph Davenport,

Mary Davenport, Thomas Davenport Sr, William Hambleton, Joseph Jenkins, Mary Jenkins, Richard Weatherford [157]

Precinct #10
Boundaries: Between Little Guinea Creek, Buckingham Road, Guinea Road, Burton's Brook, and Appomattox River [144]
Processioners: John Jones, Richard Sharp, Henry Martin, Lewis Orange
Landowners: James Arnold, William Arnold, John Burton, Williams Daniel, ?Capt. Davenport, William Davenport, John Farmer, William Hambleton, John Jones, Humphrey Keeble, Walter Keeble, Susannah Martin, Samuel Meredith, Lewis Orange, David Watson, William Watson, and others not processioned [161]

Precinct #11
Boundaries: Between Appomattox River, Burtons Brook, Guinea Road, Buckingham Road, and the road to Clements & Coxes Mill [144]
Processioners: Lawrence Smith, Richard Parker Jr, Thomas Moody, George Cox
Landowners: Archer Austin, Abraham Baker, Benjamin Bowler, John Brown, William Burton, George Cox, Henry Cox, Henry Cox Jr, Frederick Hatcher, Thomas Moody, Drusilla Parker, Richard Parker Sr, James Patteson, Richard Pringle, Royston, Lawrence Smith, Josiah Thomson, John Wayles [160]

Precinct #12
Boundaries: Between Deep Creek, the Middle Road to Salley's Path, Buckingham Road, Lyles Road, Appomattox River, Clement Mill, the road from Clement Mill to Buckingham Road, down the same to Mr. Harris' Path to John Mayo's Mill [144]
Processioners: Charles Clay, Henry Clay Jr,. Jesse Carter
Landowners: Charles Clay, Henry Clay, George Cox, John Cox, Joseph Cox, Judith Cox, Henry Cox, Williams Daniel, Martha Hughes, Francis McCraw, Poindexter Mosby, John Netherland, John Phelps, Thomas Wilkes [Wilkinson?], Joseph Woodson [171]

Precinct #13
Boundaries: Between Appomattox River, Fighting Creek, Buckingham Road, and Lyles Road [144]
Processioners: William Bailey, William Smith Joiner, Phillip Thomas Jr
Landowners: no return recorded

Precinct #14
Boundaries: Between from the fork of Fighting Creek, Randolphs Mill Creek to Buckingham
               Road, to the [South] Church, down the Creek to the fork [144]
Processioners: John Moseley, Benjamin Hatcher, Henry Clay
Landowners: Widow Blackburn, Henry Clay, George Davis, James Davis, Ned Haskins, Benjamin
               Hatcher, Charles Hatcher, Samuel Hobson, Richard Ligon, J Markham, William
               Maxey, John Mosley, Maj. Povall, John Radford, Brett Randolph deceased [168]

Precinct #15
Boundaries: Between Genito Road, the Church Road, Fighting Creek, and Appomattox River
               [144]
Processioners: John Cox, James Ligon, Thomas Moseley
Landowners: Henry Clay, William Clay, John Mosley, Thomas Mosley [164]

Precinct #16
Boundaries: Between the New Road, Buckingham Road, the Church Road, and Genito Road
               [145]
Processioners: Edward Watkins, Francis Cheatham, Abraham Baugh
Landowners: Isham Akin, William Aiken, Abraham Baugh, Joseph Baugh, Henry Clay, Peter
               Furcrun, Joel Locket, Thomas Locket, Charles Maxey, John Mosley, Thomas
               Mosley, William Mosley, Walter Scott, Edward Watkins, John Watkins, Thomas
               Watkins, Thomas Watkins Jr, Thomas Wooldridge, John Worley, William Worley
               [155]

Precinct #17
Boundaries: Between King William Parish, the New Road, Genito Road, and the county line
               [145]
Processioners: Israel Winfrey, Joseph Baugh, Lodowick Elam
Landowners: Benjamin Bailey, Alexander Bass, Christopher Bass, Abraham Baugh, James Baugh,
               Joseph Baugh, William Cheatwood, Jeremiah Hatcher, Joseph Jackson, Gideon
               Locket, Henry Moore, Arthur Mosley, John Watkins, Israel Winfrey [157]

Precinct #18
Boundaries: Between the county line, Appomattox River, and Genito Road [145]
Processioners: William Marshall, Francis Marshall, Mark Taylor
Landowners: Lodowick Elam, Creed Haskins, William Moseley deceased, Gideon Lockett, Joel
               Lockett, Thomas Lockett, Francis Marshall, William Marshall, Arthur Mosley,
               Richard Mosley, John Northcutt, Mark Taylor, John Todd, Edward Watkins, George
               Williamson deceased [156]

Precinct #19

Boundaries: Between Bollings Road, the Main Ridge Road, Buckingham Road, and the county line [145]

Processioners: Williams Daniel, John Seay, William Mills, Henry Scruggs

Landowners: Archibald Cary, Richard Barker, William Bates, James Brown, John Bullock, Peter Campbell, Church land, Daniel Coleman, James Daniel, John Daniel, Phillip Dunford, Warham Easley, Henry Garrett, Thomas Guttery, Henry Harmon, Benjamin Hendrick, Robert Kent, Maurice Langhorn, Anthony Levillion, William Mills, William Sampson, Henry Scruggs, John Seay, Joseph Starkey, John Taylor, John Telphra, Alexander Trent, Peterfield Trent, Robert Trent, James Wilkins [163]

Precinct #20

Boundaries: Between Willis River, Soakass Creek to Daniels' old houses, and Buckingham Road [145]

Processioners: Samuel Allen, Thomas Guttery, Robert Hudgens

Landowners: no return recorded

Precinct #21

Boundaries: Between Harrison's Road, the road to John Burton's Ordinary, Buckingham Road to Daniels' old houses & Soakass Creek [145]

Processioners: James Holloway, John Bowden, Isaac Beacham, William Rowton

Landowners: James Adams, Thomas Allen, William Allen, James Anderson, Mark Andrews, John Bowden, John Bradley, John Burton, James Daniel, Williams Daniel, Fuqua, William Hix, Charles Holland, William Holland, James Holloway, Orphans Holloway, Samuel Holloway, Charles Hutchison, James Meador, Jonas Meador, Samuel Milton, Richard Murray, William Rowton, Edward Tabb [153]

Precinct #22

Boundaries: Between Buckingham Road, the road from John Burton to Murray, the Courthouse Road to the Path by Stegers, to John Mayo's Mill and the Mill Path to Benjamin Harris [145]

Processioners: William Clark, Gideon Patteson, William Hobson (Little Creek), Adcock Hobson

Landowners: Richard Alderson, William Battersby deceased, John Brown, Brumskil, Chamberlin, William Clark, Joseph Fuqua, Frederick Hatcher, Henry Hatcher, John Hobson, William Hobson, William Hobson deceased, William Mattox, John Mayo, Jacob McGehee, William Meanley, Thomas Nash, Christopher Robinson, John Robinson, Robert Scruggs, Francis George Steger, Tabb, Josiah Thomson [154]

Precinct #23

Boundaries: Between the Middle Road, Randolph's Church Road, Buckingham Road, and Mr. Salley's Path [145]

Processioners: George Owen, John Burch, Benjamin Netherland

Landowners: John Barnes, Netherland Barnes, John Burch, George Cardwell, John Carrington, Hanson, William Hudspeth, Dock Hix, Henry Macon, Orphans of Mayo, Francis McCraw, McDowell, John Netherland, Thomas Osburn, George Owen, John Pleasants Sr, Richard Povall, Orphans of Randolph, Ambrose Ranson, Abraham Salley, John Hyde Saunders, Robert Smith, William Smith [161]

Precinct #24

Boundaries: Between the Middle Road, Randolph's Church Road, Buckingham Road, and the road from the Negroes Arm to Mrs. Mayo [145]

Processioners: Richard Ligon, John Baskervile, William Davis

Landowners: no return recorded

Precinct #25

Boundaries: Between Jones Creek, King William Parish lines, and Buckingham Road [145]

Processioners: Nathaniel Maxey, John Radford Jr, Peter Furcrun

Landowners: Thomas Ballow, Richard Blankenship, Susannah Epperson, Peter Furcran, Creed Haskins, Benjamin Hatcher, Sam Hatcher, Esther Langsdon, John Maxey, Nathaniel Maxey, William Maxey, John Pleasants, John Radford, John Radford Jr, Richard Radford, Humphrey Smith, James Smith, Thomas Turpin Jr, William Worley [159]

Precinct #26

Boundaries: Between Jones Creek, King William Parish lines, James River, Fine Creek to the Middle Road, the Middle Road to Mrs. Mayo, to Buckingham Road [145]

Processioners: Edward Parrott, William Watson, George Radford

Landowners: John Archer, John Baskerville, Joseph Bondurant, George Davis, James Davis, Creed Haskins, James Holeman, James Holeman deceased, Robert Hughes, Thomas Jefferson, Richard Ligon, Joseph Mayo, John Pleasants, Thomas Prosser, George Radford, John Radford, John Radford Jr, Thomas Turpin [166]

Precinct #27

Boundaries: Between the road from Michaux Ferry to Spiers' Ordinary at the Courthouse (or Middle Road), down the Middle Road to Fine Creek, down Fine Creek to James River, and up James River to the said Ferry [146]

Processioners: John Hughes, Richard James, Thomas Epperson, Bennet Goode

Landowners: Henry Bagby, John Cox, William Cox, John Fleming, Bennett Goode, Henry

Hobson, John Hughes, Martha Hughes, Richard James, Joseph Johns, Mayo, Jacob Michaux, Paul Michaux, Benjamin Netherland, John Pleasants, John Railey, orphan of William Reynolds, David Seizer, Peter Stoner, John Wilkinson, Nicholas Wilkinson, Daniel Wilmore, Charles Woodson [158]

Precinct #28
Boundaries: Between James River, the Ferry Road to Paul Michaux, the River Road, and Solomons Creek [146]
Processioners: Jacob Michaux, Daniel Johnson, James Bagby
Landowners: Henry Bagby, James Bagby, Robert Bagby, Edward Cox, John Cox, William Cox, William Fleming, John Franklin, Elizabeth Gay, Daniel Johnson, John Johnson, James Meredith, Jacob Michaux, Paul Michaux, Anthony Minter, Wade Netherland, John Hyde Saunders, John Walton, John Wilkinson, Nicholas Wilkinson, William Wilkinson, Charles Woodson [169]

Precinct #29
Boundaries: Between Deep Creek, the Middle Road, the road from Spiers to Paul Michaux, the River Road to Solomons Creek, Solomons Creek and James River [146]
Processioners: James Taylor (son of William Taylor), William Howard, Joseph Mosby, Edmond Toney
Landowners: James Bagby, Benjamin Bedford, James Bryant, David Chandler, Jesse Chandler, Robert Chandler, William Davis, William Farguson, John Franklin, George Gaddy, the Glebe, Roger Hill, William Howard, Mary Mayo, Paul Michaux, Joseph Mosby, Benjamin Netherland, John Pleasants, Thomas Randolph, Duncan Robertson (Robinson), Abraham Salley, John Hyde Saunders, William Scott, Bartholomew Stovall Sr, Bartholomew Stovall Jr, Avis Taylor, George Taylor, James Taylor, William Taylor, Edmond Toney, John Walton, Charles Woodson [170]

Precinct #30
Boundaries: Between Deep Creek, James River, Muddy Creek, and the River Road [146]
Processioners: Micajah Mosby, Charles Finch, Robert Beck
Landowners: "we have processioned and new marked all the lines" [166]

Precinct #31
Boundaries: Between Muddy Creek, as high as Scotts Mill, Scotts Road to the Middle Road, the Middle Road, Deep Creek, and the River Road [146]
Processioners: Abraham Womack, Jesse Miller, William Stratton
Landowners: Archibald Hix, Edward Morgan, Micajah Mosby, John Pleasants, John Poindexter,

Thomas Tucker, William Tucker, "all other people in our precinct say they would not have their lines processioned, they are plain enough" [168]

Precinct #32
Boundaries: Between Deep Creek, the Path to John Mayo Mill, and the Middle Road [146]
Processioners: John Cardwell, Francis George Steger, Benjamin Mosby
Landowners: no return recorded

Precinct #33
Boundaries: Between the Middle Road to Murray's Ordinary, Muddy Creek to Scott's Mill, Scott's Road to the Middle Road [146]
Processioners: Hezekiah Mosby, David Parker, John Merryman
Landowners: no return recorded

Precinct #34
Boundaries: Between Muddy Creek, James River, Willis River, and the River Road [146]
Processioners: John Woodson, William Dillon, Henry Dillon
Landowners: Edward Arms, George Carrington, Nicholas Davies, Henry Dillon, William Dillon, Robert Furlong, Carter Henry Harrison, Anne Hughes, Peter Martin, John Witch, John Woodson [169]

Precinct #35
Boundaries: Between Muddy Creek, the River Road, Carters Ferry Road, and the Chapel Road to Scotts Mill [146]
Processioners: John Murray, Drury Hudgens, John Carter (Deep Run)
Landowners: John Alexander, Charles Barker, John Carter, Bowler Cocke, John Creasy, Nicholas Davies, Henry Dillon, William Dillon, Carter Harrison, Drury Hudgens, Orlando Hughes, Richard Ligon, Peter Martin, Thomas Montague, John Murray, William Palmer, John Roland, John Scott, William Terrell, Thomas Turpin, Thomas Walton, John Woodson [152]

Precinct #36
Boundaries: Between Muddy Creek to Murray's Ordinary to Middle Road, Carters Ferry Road, and the Chapel Road [146]
Processioners: Leander Hughes Jr, Thomas Montague, William Flipping
Landowners: William Clark, Edward Clements, Bowler Cocke, Robert Douglas, James Drake, Sampson Fleming, Ralph Flipping, William Flipping, William Holland, Simon Hughes, Drury Hudgens, orphan of James Hudgens, orphan of William Hudgens,

Leander Hughes, Orlando Hughes, William Hughes deceased, Meador, John Merryman, John Merryman Jr, Thomas Montague, John Pleasants, William Sampson, Thomas Walton, John Watts, Jacob Winfrey [172]

Precinct #37

Boundaries: Between Barnard's Road, Horn Quarter Road, [Harrison's Road], and Willis River [146]

Processioners: Thomas Tabb, William Holland, John Holland

Landowners: James Anderson, John Bradley, James Brown, Samuel Brown, Orphans Butler, Charles Fleming, orphans of Benjamin Harrison, orphans of John Holland, William Holland, John Holloway, Samuel Holloway, Leonard Keeling, John Minter, Edward Tabb, Thomas Tabb [157]

Precinct #38

Boundaries: Between Carters Ferry Road, Bernard's Road, Willis River, and the River Road [147]

Processioners: John Carter Jr, John Newton, Francis Amos Jr

Landowners: Francis Amoss Sr, Francis Amoss Jr, William Allen, John Armstead, Samuel Atkinson, John Barnard, orphans of Thomas Bollings, Samuel Bridgewater, Robert Brown, Samuel Brown, John Burton, John Carter, John Carter Jr, Edmond Clements, Thomas Dews, Benjamin Dillon, William Dillon, Andrew Edwards, Benjamin Farris, Rachel Farris, James Gardian, Carter Henry Harrison, Anne Hill, John Jefferson, John Lewis, William Mason, Jonas Meador, Joel Meggs, John Newton, Samuel Oslin, Edmond Price, John Robinson, Daniel Russell, John Salmon, William Sanderson, Robert Smith, Job Thomas, John Watts, Jacob Winfrey [167]

Precinct #39

Boundaries: Between Willis River, Buckingham Road, the county line, and Randolphs Creek [147]

Processioners: Benjamin Wilson, Drury Scruggs, Robert Brown

Landowners: James Anderson, Robert Anderson, Daniel Boatwright, Robert Brown, Archibald Cary, Walthoe Daniel, Bartholomew Field, Cary Harrison, John Jude, Leonard Keeling, Nathaniel Morris, William Sampson, Drury Scruggs, James Southall, Thomas Tabb, William Terrell, Alexander Trent, George Walton, Benjamin Wilson, Joseph Woodson, Tucker Woodson [164]

Precinct #40

Boundaries: Between Willis River, Randolphs Creek, the county line, and the River Road [147]

Processioners: Phineas Glover, Isham Reynolds, Joseph Price

Landowners: Daniel Boatwright, Milton Burford, George Carrington, James Gilliam, John Glover,

Joseph Glover, Phineas Glover, Maurice Langhorn, John Lewis, Gideon Martin, Jane Martin, Orson Martin, Joseph Price, Charles Reynolds, David Reynolds, John Reynolds, William Sanderson, Alexander Trent, Drury Woodson [155]

Precinct #41
Boundaries: Between Willis River, James River, the County line, and the River Road [147]
Processioners: Samuel Taylor, Drury Woodson, Hezekiah Daverson
Landowners: William Austin, Benoni Boatwright, Jeremiah Cannon, Robert Carter, George Carrington, Hezekiah Daverson, James Gilliam (Gilham), Joseph Gilliam, Phineas Glover, Joseph Griffin, James Johnson, Joseph Johnson, John Jones, Daniel Jones, Phillip Mayo, John Meador, Burton Newton, John Parrish, David Preger, David Reynolds, James Robinson, William Rowland, Samuel Taylor, John Wayles, Drury Woodson [152]

Illustration from *Colonial Living*
by Edwin Tunis

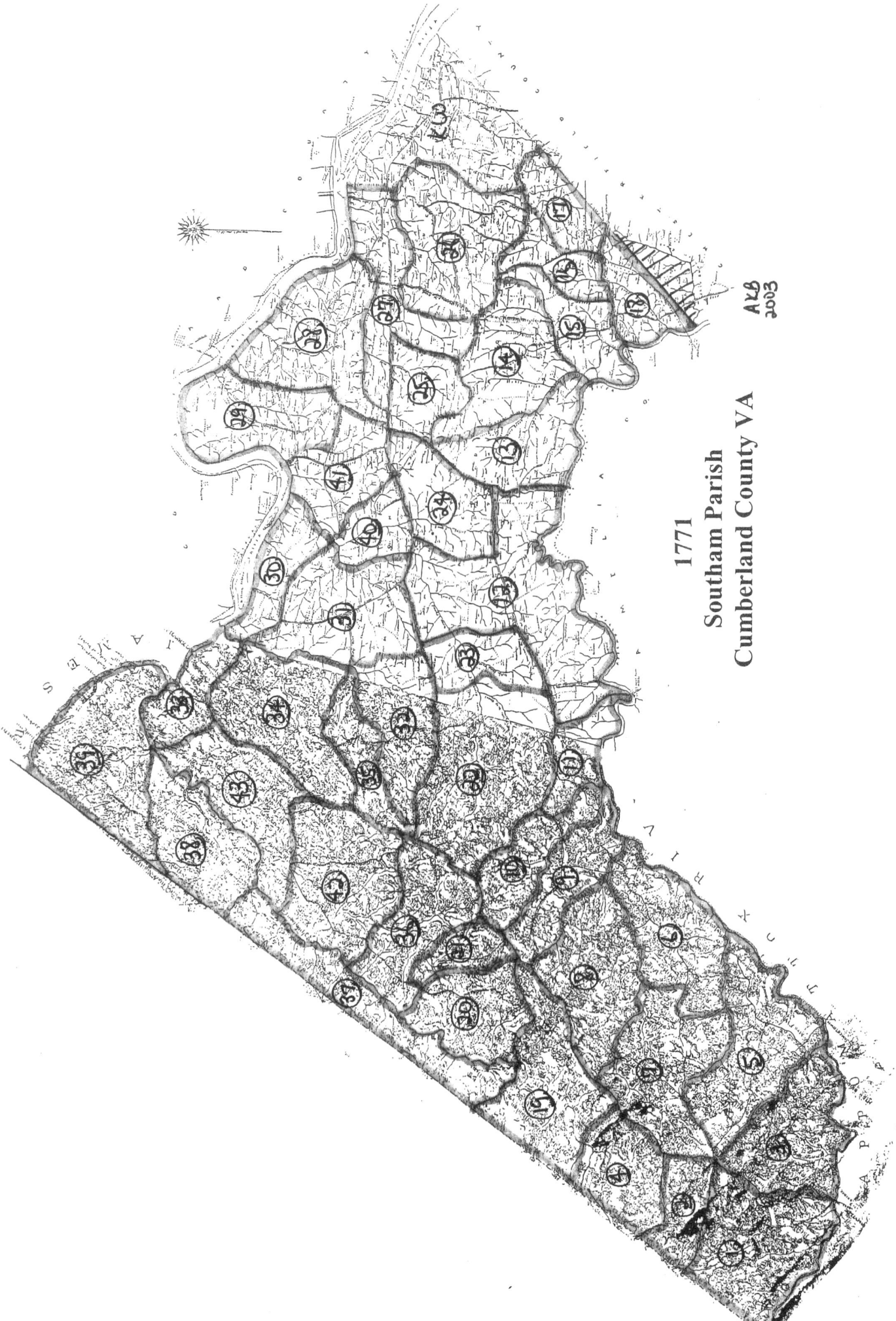

1771
Southam Parish
Cumberland County VA

ALB
2003

1771 Cumberland County

This the sixth processioning conducted for Southam Parish. The orders are dated July 29, 1771, pages [185-190], and the returns August 1, 1772, pages [194-199]. Of the 43 precincts, only 6 reported full returns for the lowest return rate of 14%. The precincts seem identified, but the boundary between #42 and $43 is new, and #32 and #35 are different.

Precinct #1
Boundaries: Between Randolph's Road, Appomattox River, the county line, and the Clover Forrest Road [185]
Processioners: Isham Richerson, Moore Lumpkin, Saymore Scott
Landowners: no return recorded

Precinct #2
Boundaries: Between Randolph's Road, the Clover Forrest Road, the county line, and Brooks Road [185]
Processioners: George Wright, Thomas Williams
Landowners: Henry Bell, Archibald Cary, Thomas Davenport, John Gannaway Sr, Robert Johns, Richard Randolph, Alexander Trent, Samuel Williams, Thomas Williams, George Wright [196]

Precinct #3
Boundaries: Between Appomattox River, Green Creek, and Randolphs Road [185]
Processioners: Joseph Michaux, William Shepard, John Chambers
Landowners: no return recorded

Precinct #4
Boundaries: Between Brooks Road, the county line, Bollings Road, and the Main Road [185]
Processioners: Thomas Word, John Colquitt, Jarrett Ellison
Landowners: Joseph Calland, Archibald Cary, John Colquitt, Charles Lee, Thomas Davenport, Alexander Stinson, Peterfield Trent, James Wilkins, Thomas Word [194]

Precinct #5
Boundaries: Between Angola Creek, Appomattox River, Green Creek, and Randolphs Road [185]
Processioners: Warren Walker, William Walker, John Holeman
Landowners: no return recorded

Precinct #6
Boundaries: Between Great Guinea Creek, Appomattox River, Angola Creek, and Col. William
                Macon's upper lines [185]
Processioners: Joshua Doss, Joseph Allen, Henry Macon
Landowners: no return recorded

Precinct #7
Boundaries: Between Col. William Macon's upper lines, Angola Creek, Randolphs Road, Glenn's
                Path to Great Guinea Creek, to the said Macon's line [185]
Processioners: William Lee, Joseph Lee, James Glenn Sr
Landowners: Joseph Anglea, William Anglea Sr, Jeremiah Basham, Davis Brown, John Brown,
                Joseph Calland, Joseph Chafin, Nathan Chafin, Stanley Chafin, Thomas Davenport,
                David Dickerson, James Durham, Francis Epperson, Gideon Glenn, James Glenn,
                Nathan Glenn, Nehemiah Glenn, James Glown, Bernard Guttery, Robert Johns,
                Thomas Johns, John Lee, Joseph Lee, Richard Lee, William Lee, Col. Macon,
                Hartwell Macon, McGehee estate, William McGehee, John Pleasants deceased,
                William Shepard, Alexander Trent, Nathan Womack, George Wright, Griffin Wright,
                John Wright, Thomas Wright [196]

Precinct #8
Boundaries: Between Tearwallet Run, Great Guinea Creek as high as Glenn's Path, and the Main
                Ridge Road [186]
Processioners: Mark Andrews, Daniel Allen, John Noel
Landowners: no return recorded

Precinct #9
Boundaries: Between Little Guinea Creek, Appomattox River, Great Guinea Creek, Tearwallet
                Run, and the Main Ridge Road [186]
Processioners: William Davenport, William Hambleton, William Major, Benjamin Sims
Landowners: no return recorded

Precinct #10
Boundaries: Between Little Guinea Creek, Buckingham Road, Guinea Road, Burtons Brook, and
                Appomattox River [186]
Processioners: John Jones, Henry Martin, John Burton
Landowners: no return recorded

Precinct #11

Boundaries: Between Appomattox River, Burtons Brook, Guinea Road, Buckingham Road, and the Road to Clements and Coxes Mill [186]

Processioners: William Allen, Burton, Thomas Moody, George Cox

Landowners: no return recorded

Precinct #12

Boundaries: Between Appomattox River, Clements Mills path, Buckingham Road, the Cross Road by Mr. Swann to the Middle Road, to Salley's Path, to Buckingham Road, to Lyles Road, to Appomattox River [186]

Processioners: Poindexter Mosby, Jesse Carter, Robert Moore

Landowners: no return recorded

Precinct #13

Boundaries: Between Fighting Creek, Buckingham Road, Lyles Road, and Appomattox River [186]

Processioners: William Smith Joiner, William Elam, Charles Lewis

Landowners: no return recorded

Precinct #14

Boundaries: Between from the fork of Fighting Creek, Randolphs Mill Creek to Buckingham Road, to the [South] Church, down the Creek to the fork [186]

Processioners: Richard Eggleston, Samuel Hobson, George Davis

Landowners: no return recorded

Precinct #15

Boundaries: Between Genito Road, Church Road, Fighting Creek, and Appomattox River [187]

Processioners: George Williamson, John Moseley, Thomas Moseley

Landowners: no return recorded

Precinct #16

Boundaries: Between the New Road, Genito Road, the Church Road, and Buckingham Road [187]

Processioners: Edward Watkins, Abraham Baugh, Edward Watkins Jr

Landowners: no return recorded

Precinct #17
Boundaries: Between King William Parish, [Buckingham Road], the new Road, Genito Road, and
                 the county line [187]
Processioners: Israel Winfrey, Joseph Baugh, Lodowick Elam
Landowners: no return recorded

Precinct #18
Boundaries: Between the county line, Appomattox River, and Genito Road [187]
Processioners: Arthur Moseley, Edward Haskins, John Todd
Landowners: no return recorded

Precinct #19
Boundaries: Between Bollings Road, the main Ridge Road, Buckingham Road, and the county
                 line [187]
Processioners: Matthew Sims, John Seay, Alexander Guttery
Landowners: Francis Amoss, Charles Barker, James Brown, Joseph Calland, Thomas Calwell,
                 Archibald Cary, Daniel Coleman, William Coleman, Jonathan Colquitt, Williams
                 Daniel, William Dunge, Warham Easley, Farris, John Farmer, Henry Garrett, James
                 Garrett, Alexander Guttery, Thomas Guttery, William Guttery, Zachariah Hendrick,
                 Dennitt Hill, John Hill, Thomas Hill, Thomas Johns Sr, Maurice Langhorne, John
                 McKinney, Benjmain Mosby, Jesse Sanders, Henry Scruggs, John Seay, Matthew
                 Sims, James Southall, John Spearman, John Starkey, Darby Tarlyle, Alexander Trent,
                 Peterfield Trent, Benjamin Weaver, Stephen Woodson [194]

Precinct #20
Boundaries: Between Willis River, Soakass Creek, Daniels old houses, and Buckingham Road
                 [187]
Processioners: Moses Hudgens, William Coleman, Charles Barker
Landowners: no return recorded

Precinct #21
Boundaries: Between Harrison Road, the road to John Burton's Ordinary, Buckingham Road, and
                 Soakass Creek, [Willis River] [187]
Processioners: John Bradley, Thomas Holland, Thomas Bartee
Landowners: no return recorded

Precinct #22
Boundaries: Between Buckingham Road, the road from John Burton to Overton's Ordinary, the Courthouse Road, to William Clark's Path, by the said Clark and Richard Alderson, Hobsons Mill Path, to Buckingham Road [187]
Processioners: John Hobson, Field Robinson, Edward Robinson
Landowners: no return recorded

Precinct #23
Boundaries: Between Buckingham Road, Hobsons Mill Path by Richard Aldersons and William Clark to the Courthouse Road, the Courthouse Road and the crossroad by Mr. Swann to Buckingham Road [188]
Processioners: William Clerk, Joseph Harris, John Steger
Landowners: no return recorded

Precinct #24
Boundaries: Between the Middle Road, Randolphs Church Road, Buckingham Road, and Salley's Path [188]
Processioners: Francis McCraw, Hughes Woodson, John Hyde Sanders
Landowners: no return recorded

Precinct #25
Boundaries: Between the Middle Road, Lyles Road, Buckingham Road, and the Road from the Negroes Arm to Mrs. Mayo [188]
Processioners: Richard Ligon, George Radford, Richard Radford
Landowners: no return recorded

Precinct #26
Boundaries: Between Jones Creek, King William Parish lines, and Buckingham Road
Processioners: Thomas Ballow, Thomas Haskins, Charles Hatcher
Landowners: no return recorded

Precinct #27
Boundaries: Between Jones Creek, King William Parish lines, James River, Fine Creek, Middle Road, Mrs. Mayo, and Buckingham Road [188]
Processioners: Joseph Bondurant, William Watson, Edward Parrott
Landowners: John Baskerville, Samuel Baskerville, Joseph Bondurant, Anthony Christian, Richard Ligon, Joseph Mayo, John Pleasants deceased, George Radford, Richard Radford [198]

Precinct #28
Boundaries: Between the road from Michaux Ferry, Woodson's Plantation on the Middle Road,
                Fine Creek, down Fine Creek to James River, up James River to the said Ferry [188]
Processioners: Bennet Goode, John Hughes, Peter Stoner
Landowners: no return recorded

Precinct #29
Boundaries: Between James River, the Ferry Road to Stoners? Ordinary, the River Road and
                Solomon Creek [188]
Processioners: Anthony Minter, John Cox, Edward Cox
Landowners: no return recorded

Precinct #30
Boundaries: Between Deep Creek, James River, Muddy Creek, and the River Road [189]
Processioners: Micajah Mosby, Patrick Fitzsimmons, Richard Baskerville
Landowners: no return recorded

Precinct #31
Boundaries: Between Muddy Creek as high as Scotts Mill, Scotts Road, the Middle Road, [Deep
                Creek], and the River Road [189]
Processioners: Nicholas Spiers, Charles Scott, Edmond Logwood
Landowners: no return recorded

Precinct #32
Boundaries: Between the Middle Road to Overton's Ordinary, Muddy Creek to Scott's Mill,
                Scott's Road to the Middle Road [189]
Processioners: Hezekiah Daniel, Mosby?, David Parker
Landowners: no return recorded

Precinct #33
Boundaries: Between Muddy Creek, James River, Willis River, and River Road [189]
Processioners: Carter Henry Harrison, Henry Landon Davies, John Woodson
Landowners: no return recorded

Precinct #34
Boundaries: Between Muddy Creek, the River Road, Carter Ferry Road, and the Church Road to
                Scott's Mill [189]

Processioners: Thomas Walton, John Murray, Nicholas Mosby
Landowners: no return recorded

Precinct #35
Boundaries: Between Muddy Creek, John Overton's Ordinary, [at] the Middle Road, Carters
              Ferry Road, and the Church Road [189]
Processioners: John Flipping, Simon Hughes, James Hudgens, Francis Flipping
Landowners: no return recorded

Precinct #36
Boundaries: Between Bernard's Road, Hornquarter Road, and Willis River [189]
Processioners: George Keeling, Samuel Powel, Thomas Smith
Landowners: no return recorded

Precinct #37
Boundaries: Between Willis River, Buckingham Road, the county line, and Randolphs Creek
              [189]
Processioners: Benjamin Wilson, Drury Scruggs, Daniel Boatwright, Robert Brown
Landowners: no return recorded

Precinct #38
Boundaries: Between Willis River, Randolphs Creek, the county line, and River Road
Processioners: John Newton, Austin Martin, Phineas Glover Jr
Landowners: no return recorded

Precinct #39
Boundaries: Between Willis River, James River, the county line, and River Road [189]
Processioners: Drury Woodson, James Gilliam, Hezekiah Davison
Landowners: no return recorded

Precinct #40
Boundaries: Between Deep Creek, the Middle Road, to Stewarts, the road from Stewart to the
              Widow Chandler, the road from the Widow Chandler to the River Road above
              Duncan Robinson, and River Road [190]
Processioners: Benjamin Bedford, Joseph Mosley, Robert Scruggs
Landowners: no return recorded

Precinct #41

Boundaries: Between the Middle Road, the road from Charles Woodson's Quarter to Stoner's Ordinary, the River Road, Solomons Creek, James River, Deep Creek, the River Road, down the Road above Duncan Robinson to the Widow Chandler, the said Road, and the road from the Widow Chandler to Stewart [190]

Processioners: James Pleasants, Bartholomew Stovall Jr, Edmond Toney

Landowners: no return recorded

Precinct #42

Boundaries: Between Willis River, Bernard's Road, Carters Ferry Road, the Church Road to the Church, down the Church Spring branch and Turkey Cock Run to the Creek [190]

Processioners: Martin Richardson, Jonas Meador, William Sanderson

Landowners: Archer Allen, Archibald Allen, James Austin, Daniel Boatwright, Page Bond deceased, Samuel Bridgewater, James Brown, Samuel Brown, Edward Clements, Edward Coleman, Allen Criddle, James Daniel, Andrew Edwards, Andrew Edwards Jr, William Edwards, James Foster, Parson Garden, William C. Hill, John Hix, James Hudgens, James Hudson, John Jefferson, Farrett Lyle, James Meador, Joel Meggs, James Minter, John Minter, Jesse Oslin, Samuel Oslin deceased, Martin Richardson, John Robertson, William Sanderson, Thomas Smith, Job Thomas, Alexander Trent, Henry Wade [198]

Precinct #43

Boundaries: Between Willis River, the River Road, Carters Ferry Road, the Church upper Road, to the [Ham] Church, and down the Spring branch to Willis [190]

Processioners: Francis Amoss, John Armstead, Simon Roland

Landowners: no return recorded

Illustration from *Colonial Living*
by Edwin Tunis

1775, 1779, 1783
Cumberland, Powhatan Co VA

1775 Cumberland County

This was the seventh processioning in Southam Parish, but the first after Littleton Parish was removed. The number of precincts has been reduced from 43 to 19. The precincts were assigned on August 19, 1775, pages [205-207]. No returns were recorded. All of the precincts are clearly identified and remained unchanged for the next 2 processionings.

Precinct #1
Boundaries: Between Fighting Creek, Buckingham Road, Lyles Road and the Appomattox River [205]
Processioners: Philip Thomas, William Elam, Charles Lewis

Precinct #2
Boundaries: Between Genito Road, the Church Road to Fighting Creek, and the Appomattox River [205]
Processioners: George Williamson, John Mosley Jr, Thomas Mosley

Precinct #3
Boundaries: From the Fork of Fighting Creek, Randolph's Mill Creek, to Buckingham Road, down the same to the [South] Church, down the Creek to the Fork [205]
Processioners: Richard Eggleston, Samuel Hobson, George Davis

Precinct #4
Boundaries: Between the new Road, Genito Road, the Church Road, and Buckingham Road
Processioners: Edward Watkins, Abraham Baugh, Edward Watkins Jr

Precinct #5
Boundaries: Between King William Parish, the New Road, Genito Road, and the county line [205]
Processioners: Israel Winfrey, Joseph Baugh, Lodowick Elam

Precinct #6
Boundaries: Between the county line, the Appomattox River, and Genito Road [205]
Processioners: Arthur Mosley, Robert Williamson, Edward Haskins, John Cox

Precinct #7

Boundaries: Between the Middle Road, Randolph's Church Road, Buckingham Road and the Road from Salley's Plantation to Buckingham Road [205]

Processioners: Hughes Woodson, David Owen, John Barnes

Precinct #8

Boundaries: Between the Middle Road, Lyles Road, Buckingham Road and the Road from the Negroes Arm to Mr. Joseph Mayo [205]

Processioners: Joseph Mayo, George Radford, John Ligon

Precinct #9

Boundaries: Between Jones Creek, the King William Parish Line, Buckingham Road and the lower end of the parish [206]

Processioners: Thomas Ballow, Charles Hatcher, Thomas Haskins, John Maxey

Precinct #10

Boundaries: Between Jones Creek, the King William Parish line, and James River, Fine Creek to the Middle Road, Middle Road to Mr. Joseph Mayo, Mr. Joseph Mayo's Road to Buckingham Road [206]

Processioners: Nathaniel Maxey, William Watson, Edward Parrott, Aaron Haskins

Precinct #11

Boundaries: Between the Road from Michaux Ferry to Charles Woodson's Plantation, on the Middle Road down the same to Fine Creek, down Fine Creek to the James River, up the James River to Michaux Ferry [206]

Processioners: Bennett Goode, Edmund Vaughan, John Goode, Peter Stoner

Precinct #12

Boundaries: Between the James River, the Ferry Road to Robert Murray's Store, [River Road], and Solomons Creek [206]

Processioners: Anthony Minter, John Cox, Edward Cox

Precinct #13

Boundaries: Between Deep Creek, the James River, the Parish line, and River Road [206]

Processioners: Jesse Mosby, Daniel Hix, Robert Murray

Precinct #14
Boundaries: From Deep Creek, the Middle Road, down Loyd's, the Road from Loyd's to Edmund Toney's, the road from Edmund Toney's to the River Road above Duncan Robertson's, and River Road [206]
Processioners: William Mayo, James Drake, Edmund Toney Jr

Precinct #15
Boundaries: Between the Middle Road, the road from Charles Woodson's to Robert Murray's Store, the River Road, Solomon's Creek, James River, Deep Creek, the River Road, down the road above Duncan Robinson's to Edmund Toney's, and the road from Edmund Toney's to Loyd's [206]
Processioners: James Pleasants, Bartholomew Stovall Jr, Charles Woodson Jr

Precinct #16
Boundaries: Between Thomas Moody, the parish line on Appomattox River to Swann's Creek, Buckingham Road, up Buckingham Road to the parish line, the parish line to the beginning [206]
Processioners: George Cox, Henry Cox, Williams Daniel

Precinct #17
Boundaries: Between Swann's Creek and Appomattox River, down the River to Lyles Ford, along Lyles Road to Buckingham Road, up the road to Swann's Creek [207]
Processioners: Poindexter Mosby, Jesse Carter, Robert Biscoe

Precinct #18
Boundaries: Between the parish line on Buckingham Road to the Middle Road, down the Middle Road to Salley's Path, Buckingham Road, up Buckingham Road to the parish line, along that to the beginning [207]
Processioners: Joseph Harris, John Steger, Thomas Steger, Hans Steger

Precinct #19
Boundaries: Between Muddy Creek, the parish line, to the Middle Road, Deep Creek, and the River Road [207]
Processioners: Jesse Miller, William Tucker, John Stratton, William Stratton Jr

1779 Cumberland County

This was the eighth processioning for Southam Parish. The precincts were ordered on September 24, 1779, pages [213-216], the returns are dated October 10, 1780, pages [218-224]. Of the 19 precincts, there are returns for 9 precincts for a 47% rate. All of the precincts are clearly identified.

Precinct #1
Boundaries: Between Fighting Creek, Buckingham Road, Lyle's Road, and Appomattox River
Processioners: John Povall, Charles Lewis, William Elam [213]
Landowners: William Archer, J P Baugh, John Baugh, William Elam, Charles Lewis, Stokes McCall, Charles Povall, John Povall, Richard Povall, Peyton Randolph, Phillip Thomas, David Thomson [222]

Precinct #2
Boundaries: Between Genito Road, the Church Road to Fighting Creek, and Appomattox River
Processioners: George Williamson, Robert Williamson, John Moseley Jr [213]
Landowners: "we have processioned all the lines in our precinct, the people all present or consenting" [223]

Precinct #3
Boundaries: Between from the fork of Fighting Creek, Randolphs Mill Creek to Buckingham Road, down the road to the Church, down the Creek to the fork [213]
Processioners: Samuel Hobson, George Davis, Charles Povall
Landowners: Thomas Ballow, William Blackburn, James Bransford, Anthony Christian, Anthony Christian Jr, Elijah Clay, George Davis, Richard Eggleston, Joel Fuqua, Charles Harris, Benjamin Hatcher, Charles Hatcher, William Hatcher, Samuel Hobson, Seth Ligon, William Macon, William Mosley, John Pittman, Charles Povall, George Radford, Brett Randolph estate, Peyton Randolph, Jesse Roper, Peter Wilkinson [218]

Precinct #4
Boundaries: Between the New Road, Genito Road, the Church Road, and Buckingham Road
Processioners: Edward Watkins Jr, Abraham Baugh, Henry Watkins [213]
Landowners: Abraham Baugh, James Bransford, Peter Day, John Dean, Matthew Farley, Mrs. Jones, Arthur Mosley, John Moseley, Thomas Moseley, John Pankey, William Reynolds, Alexander Trent, John Vest, Edward Watkins Sr, Edward Watkins Jr, John Watkins [222]

Precinct #5
Boundaries: Between King William Parish line, the New Road, Genito Road, and the county line
Processioners: John Pankey, Arthur Moseley Sr, Henry Moore [213]
Landowners: Christopher Bass, Abraham Baugh, Rachel Baugh, John Burton, William Cheatwood, Eleazer Clay, Peter Depp, Matthew Farley, John Fowler, John Fowler Jr, Henry Hatcher, James Hill, Joseph Jackson, William Johnson, Gideon Lockett, William Marshall, Henry Moore, Arthur Mosley, Benjamin Mosley, John Pankey, William Reynolds, Mark Taylor, Alexander Trent, Edward Watkins, Edmond Wooldridge, William Wooldridge [220]

Precinct #6
Boundaries: Between the county line, Appomattox River, and Genito Road [214]
Processioners: Gideon Locket, Arthur Mosley, Francis Marshall
Landowners: "we have processioned all the lines in our precinct, the people all consenting" [218]

Precinct #7
Boundaries: Between the Middle Road, Randolphs Church Road, Buckingham Road, and the Road from Abraham Salley's Plantation to Buckingham Road [214]
Processioners: Crutcher Baugh, John Baugh, Richard Eggleston Sr
Landowners: no return recorded

Precinct #8
Boundaries: Between the Middle Road, Lyles Road, Buckingham Road, and the Road from the Negroes Arm to Joseph Mayo's [214]
Processioners: John Ligon, Thomas Colwell, Charles Woodson Sr
Landowners: no return recorded

Precinct #9
Boundaries: Between Jones Creek, King William Parish line, Buckingham Road, and the lower end of the parish [214]
Processioners: Richard Radford, John Maxey, Charles Hatcher
Landowners: "we have processioned all the lands contained in our bounds" [220]

Precinct #10
Boundaries: Between Jones Creek, King William Parish line, James River, Fine Creek to the Middle Road, Middle Road to Joseph Mayo's, Joseph Mayo's Road to Buckingham Road [214]
Processioners: William Watson, George Radford, Aaron Haskins

Landowners: Henry Archer, William Archer, William Bagby, Anthony Christian, Richard
               Cumpton, Joel Fuqua, John Jude, Seth Ligon, William Mosley, Miriam Pleasants,
               Robert Pleasants, Samuel Pleasants, George Radford, Thomas Turpin [219]

Precinct #11
Boundaries: Between the road from Michaux Ferry to Charles Woodson's plantation on the
               Middle Road, down the same to Fine Creek, down Fine Creek to James River, up
               James River to the Ferry [214]
Processioners: Edmund Vaughn, Bennet Goode, William Reynolds, Joseph Mayo
Landowners: no return recorded

Precinct #12
Boundaries: Between James River, the Ferry Road to Prosser's Ordinary, the River Road, and
               Solomon's Creek [215]
Processioners: Edward Cox, Samuel H. Saunders, James Bagby
Landowners: Henry Bagby, James Bagby, Burrell Baugh, William Carr, William Clark, Edward
               Cox, John Cox, William Cox, William Fleming, William Gay, William Kerr, Joseph
               Ligon, Joel Owen, Anthony Minter, Samuel H. Saunders, Edmund Vaughn, James
               Wilkinson, John Wilkinson, Thomas Wilkinson, Samuel Woodson, Paul Wright
               [223]

Precinct #13
Boundaries: Between Deep Creek, Muddy Creek, James River, the parish line, and River Road
               [215]
Processioners: Robert Hughes, Robert Murray, Daniel Hix
Landowners: Thomas Bolling, Archibald Hix, Daniel Hix, David Hughes, Robert Hughes, Charles
               Logan, Richard Minter, Jesse Mosby, Robert Murray, John Stewart, William
               Stratton, John Swann, Thomas Tucker Jr, Jesse Tucker, William Tucker [219]

Precinct #14
Boundaries: Between Deep Creek, the Middle Road, down to Loyd's, the road from Loyds to
               Edmond Toney, the Road from Edmond Toney to the River Road above Duncan
               Robertson, and the River Road [215]
Processioners: James Drake, Edmond Toney Jr, Robert Taylor
Landowners: "we have processioned all the lands within our bounds" [221]

Precinct #15
Boundaries: Between the Middle Road, the Road from Charles Woodson to Prosser's Ordinary, the River Road, Solomon Creek, James River, Deep Creek, the River Road, down the Road above Duncan Robertson to Edmond Toney & the said Road from Edmond Toney to Loyds [215]
Processioners: Charles Woodson Jr, Bartholomew Stovall, Edmond Toney
Landowners: no return recorded

Precinct #16
Boundaries: Between Thomas Moody, the parish line on Appomattox River to Swanns Creek & so to Buckingham Road, up the said road to the parish line, the parish line to the beginning [215]
Processioners: Langhorn Tabb, Archelus Nunnally, Henry Cox Sr
Landowners: James Bradley, James Bradley estate, William A. Burton, William Clements, George Cox, Henry Cox, William Cox, Williams Daniel, Robert Gordon, Edward Harris, Francis E. Harris, Henry Hatcher, Thomas Moody, Archelus Nunnally, Edward Munford, Henry Skipwith, Langhorn Tabb [223]

Precinct #17
Boundaries: Between Swann's Creek & Appomattox River, down the River to Lyle's Ford, along Lyle's Road to Buckingham Road, up the road to Swann's Creek [215]
Processioners: Francis E. Harris, Robert Biscoe, Poindexter Mosby
Landowners: Francis Barber, Robert Biscoe, James R. Bradley estate, Charles Clay, Bartlett Colley, Richard Crump, J Drake, Ann Harris, Francis E. Harris, Samuel Hobson, Thomas Howlett, Charles Lewis, Vincent Markham, William Mayo, Mary McCraw, Robert Moore, Poindexter Mosby, Patteson estate, Richard Povall, Robert Smith, Philip Thomas, Hughes Woodson, Joseph Woodson [221]

Precinct #18
Boundaries: Between the parish line on Buckingham Road, to the Middle Road, down the Middle Road to Salley's Path, to Buckingham Road, up Buckingham Road to the parish line, along that to the beginning [215]
Processioners: Thomas Steger, Hans Steger, Francis Steger, Joseph Harris
Landowners: no return recorded

Precinct #19
Boundaries: Between Muddy Creek, the parish line to the Middle Road, Deep Creek, and River Road [216]
Processioners: Edmond Logwood, John Moss, Nicholas Spiers
Landowners: no return recorded

1783 Powhatan County

This was the ninth and final processioning in Southam Parish and the first one done after the American Revolution. The precincts were assigned on November 6, 1783, pages [228-231]. No returns were recorded. All of the precincts are clearly identified and remained unchanged from 1775.

Precinct #1
Boundaries: Between Fighting Creek, Buckingham Road, Lyles Road, and Appomattox River
Processioners: John Povall, William Elam, Field Archer

Precinct #2
Boundaries: Between Genito Road, the Church Road, Fighting Creek, and Appomattox River
Processioners: John Moseley Jr, Benjamin Mosby, Edward Watkins Sr

Precinct #3
Boundaries: Between the fork of Fighting Creek, Randolphs Mill Creek to Buckingham Road,
                down the same to the [South] Church, down the Creek to the Fork
Processioners: Samuel Hobson, George Davis, Charles Povall

Precinct #4
Boundaries: Between the New Road, Genito Road, the Church Road, and Buckingham Road
Processioners: Edward Watkins Jr, Abraham Baugh, Matthew Farley Sr

Precinct #5
Boundaries: Between King William Parish, the new road, Genito Road, and the county line
Processioners: Seth Hatcher, Arthur Moseley Sr, Henry Moore

Precinct #6
Boundaries: Between the county line, Appomattox River, and Genito Road
Processioners: Gideon Locket, Arthur Mosley, William Mosley

Precinct #7
Boundaries: Between the Middle Road, Randolphs Church Road, Buckingham Road and the road
                that leads from Salley's Plantation to Buckingham Road
Processioners: Crutcher Baugh, John Eggleston, Jacob Williamson

Precinct #8

Boundaries: Between the Middle Road, Lyles Road, Buckingham Road, and the road from the Negroes Arm Road to Joseph Mayo's

Processioners: John Ligon, Seth Ligon, William Macon

Precinct #9

Boundaries: Between Jones Creek, King William Parish line, Buckingham Road and the lower end of the parish

Processioners: Peter Pollock, John Maxey, Charles Hatcher

Precinct #10

Boundaries: Between Jones Creek, King William Parish line, and James River, Fine Creek to the Middle Road, Middle Road to Joseph Mayo's, Joseph Mayo's Road to Buckingham Road

Processioners: George Radford, Gideon Flournoy, Benjamin Jude

Precinct #11

Boundaries: Between the road from Michaux Ferry to Charles Woodson's plantation on the Middle Road, down the same to Fine Creek, down Fine Creek to the James River, up the James River to Michaux Ferry

Processioners: Bennett Goode, Joseph Mayo, John Good

Precinct #12

Boundaries: Between James River, the Ferry Road to Prosser's Ordinary, [River Road], and Solomon's Creek

Processioners: John Cox, John Baugh, James Bagby

Precinct #13

Boundaries: Between Deep Creek, James River, the Parish line, and River Road

Processioners: Robert Hughes, Daniel Hix, Edward Hix

Precinct #14

Boundaries: Between Deep Creek, the Middle Road, down to Loyds, the Road from Loyds to Edmond Toneys, the road from Edmond Toneys to the River Road above Duncan Robertson, and River Road

Processioners: Edmond Toney Jr, Robert Taylor, James Taylor

Precinct #15

Boundaries: Between the Middle Road, the road from Charles Woodson's to Prosser's Ordinary, the River Road, Solomon's Creek, James River, Deep Creek, the River Road, down to the Road above Duncan Robertsons to Edmond Toneys, and the said road from Edmond Toneys to Loyds

Processioners: Edmond Toney Sr, Charles Woodson Jr, Batt Stovall

Precinct #16

Boundaries: Between Thomas Moody's, the Parish line on Appomattox River, to Swan's Creek to Buckingham Road, up the said road to the parish lines, the parish line to the beginning

Processioners: Langhorn Tabb, Archelaus Nunnally, Edward Munford

Precinct #17

Boundaries: Between Swan's Creek and Appomattox River, down the River to Lyles Ford, along Lyles Road to Buckingham Road up the said road to Swans Creek

Processioners: Francis E. Harris, Robert Biscoe, Edward Harris

Precinct #18

Boundaries: Between the parish line on Buckingham Road to the Middle Road, down the Middle Road to Salley's Path, to Buckingham Road, up Buckingham Road to the parish line, along that to beginning

Processioners: Thomas Steger, Hans Steger, Joseph Harris

Precinct #19

Boundaries: Between Muddy Creek, the Parish line to the Middle Road, Deep Creek, and the River Road

Processioners: Edmond Logwood, Robert Mosby, Nicholas Spiers

Historical Maps
of
Southam Parish

1745
Goochland County
St. James Northam, St. James Southam, King William Parishes

Map by permission of Eric Grundset
Historical Boundary Atlas of Central Virginia

1749
Cumberland County
Southam Parish

Map by permission of Eric Grundset
Historical Boundary Atlas of Central Virginia

Southam Parish 1745-1772

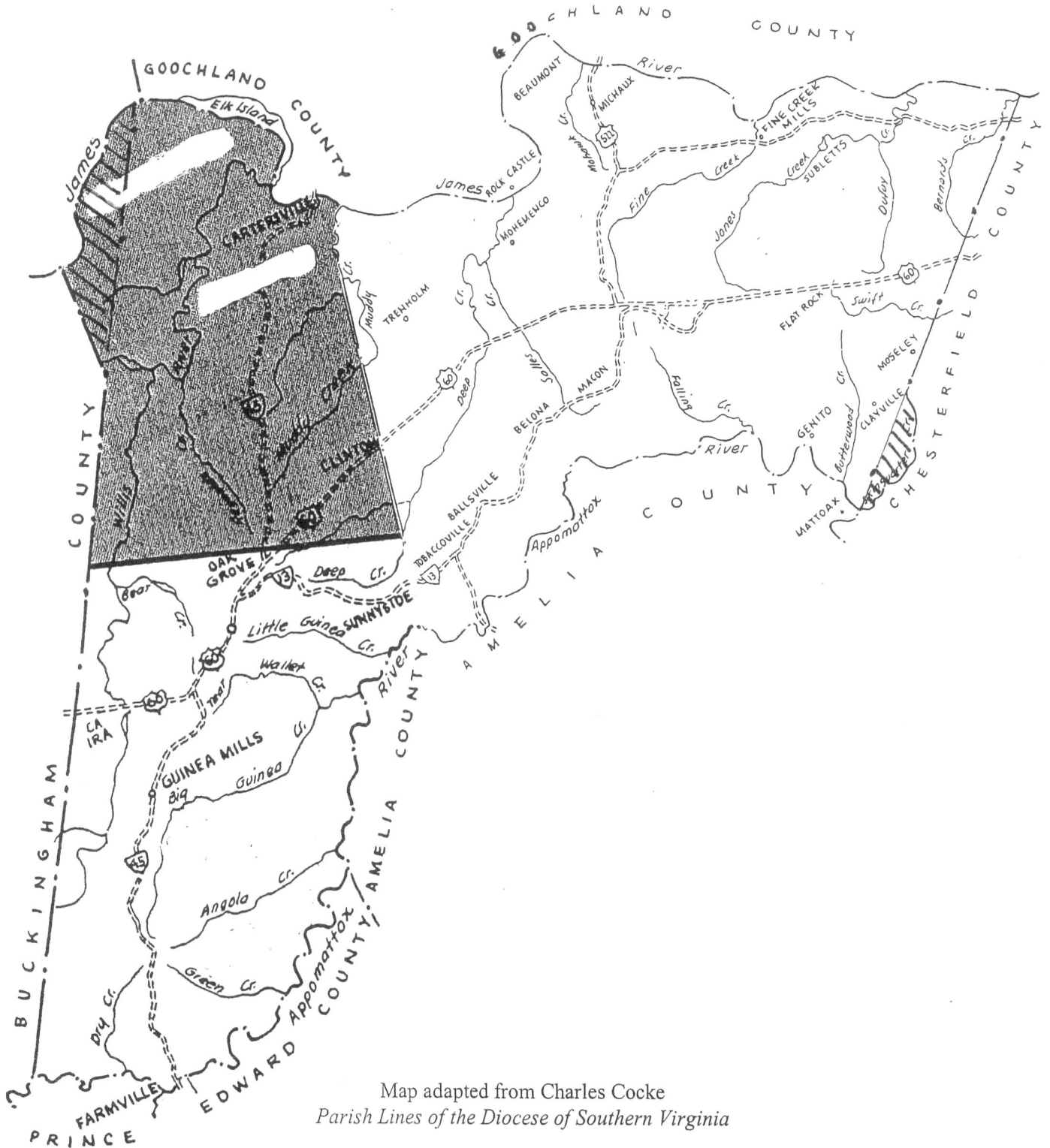

Map adapted from Charles Cocke
Parish Lines of the Diocese of Southern Virginia

Southam Parish 1772-1792

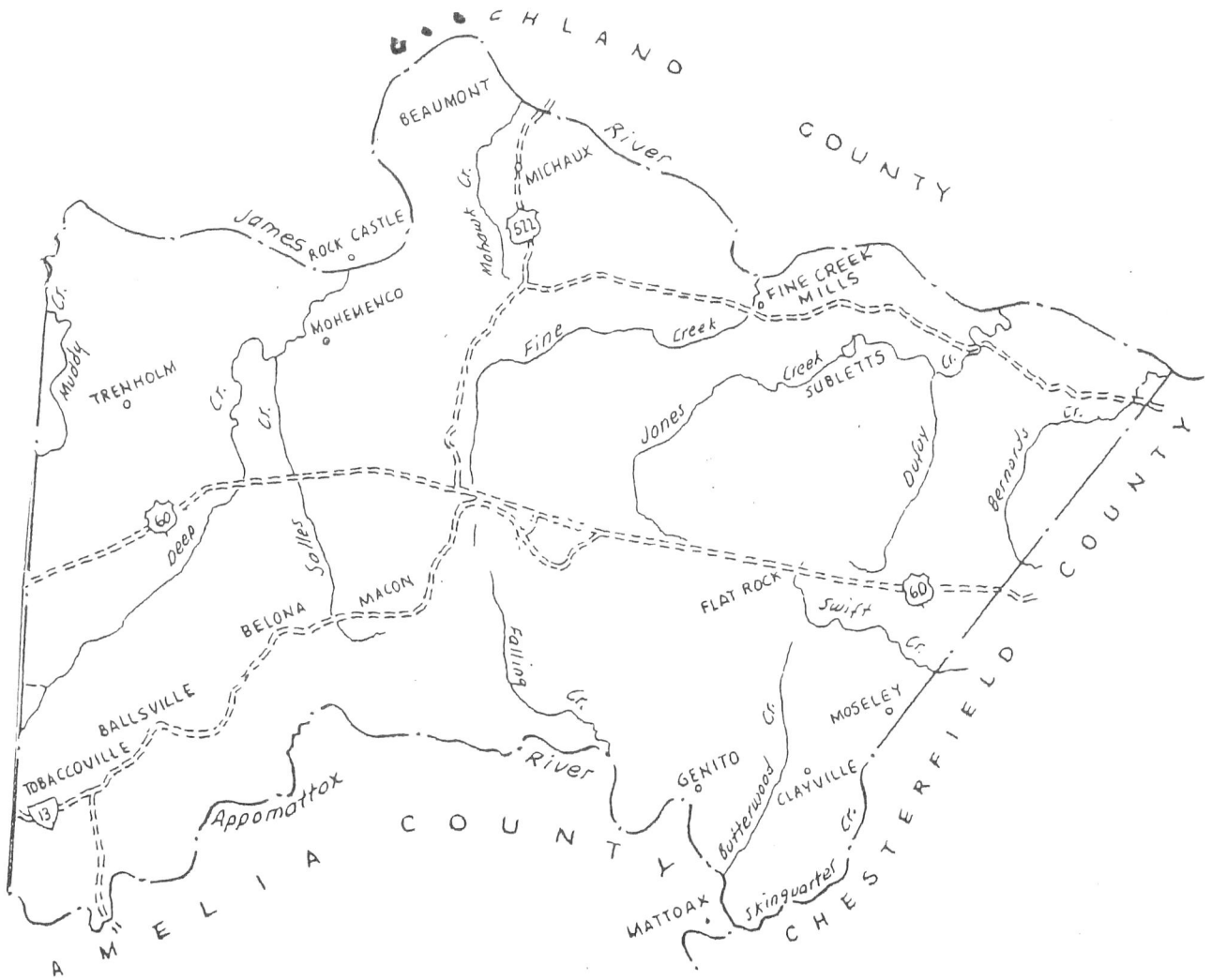

Map adapted from Charles Cocke
Parish Lines of the Diocese of Southern Virginia

The 1777 Map

In 1777, the residents of the eastern half of Cumberland County petitioned the Virginia General Assembly for a new county to be called Powhatan. Since the dividing line between Southam Parish and Littleton Parish had been a successful separation in 1772, the same line was used to divide the counties.

Probably as part of the petition to the Assembly, a map of Cumberland County was drawn in 1777, showing the proposed dividing line and some landmarks.[9] This map is a very early county map in the collection of the Library of Virginia. Interestingly, the map is drawn "upside down" with north at the bottom of the page and south at the top. This map clearly shows the original shape of Cumberland County with completely straight eastern and western county boundaries. The following is written on the map:

The computed diffrance from the court house to the upper point is thirty five miles, and to the lesser point is now more than Twenty two, in the upper Point are chiefly Negro Quarters there very few white People there more than twenty five Miles from the Court house.

Bridges in the upper Parish are over
Great Guinea	1
Little Guinea	2
Willies's Creek	2
and soon accepted 1 more	
part of Muddy Creek	1
near 3/4 of two over Appamattox	
another over Willis's Cr	

Bridges in the lower Parish are over
Jones's Creek	1
Deep Creek	2
Muddy Creek	1
D°. part of another	1
part of 1 over Appamattox	
over Butter Wood	1

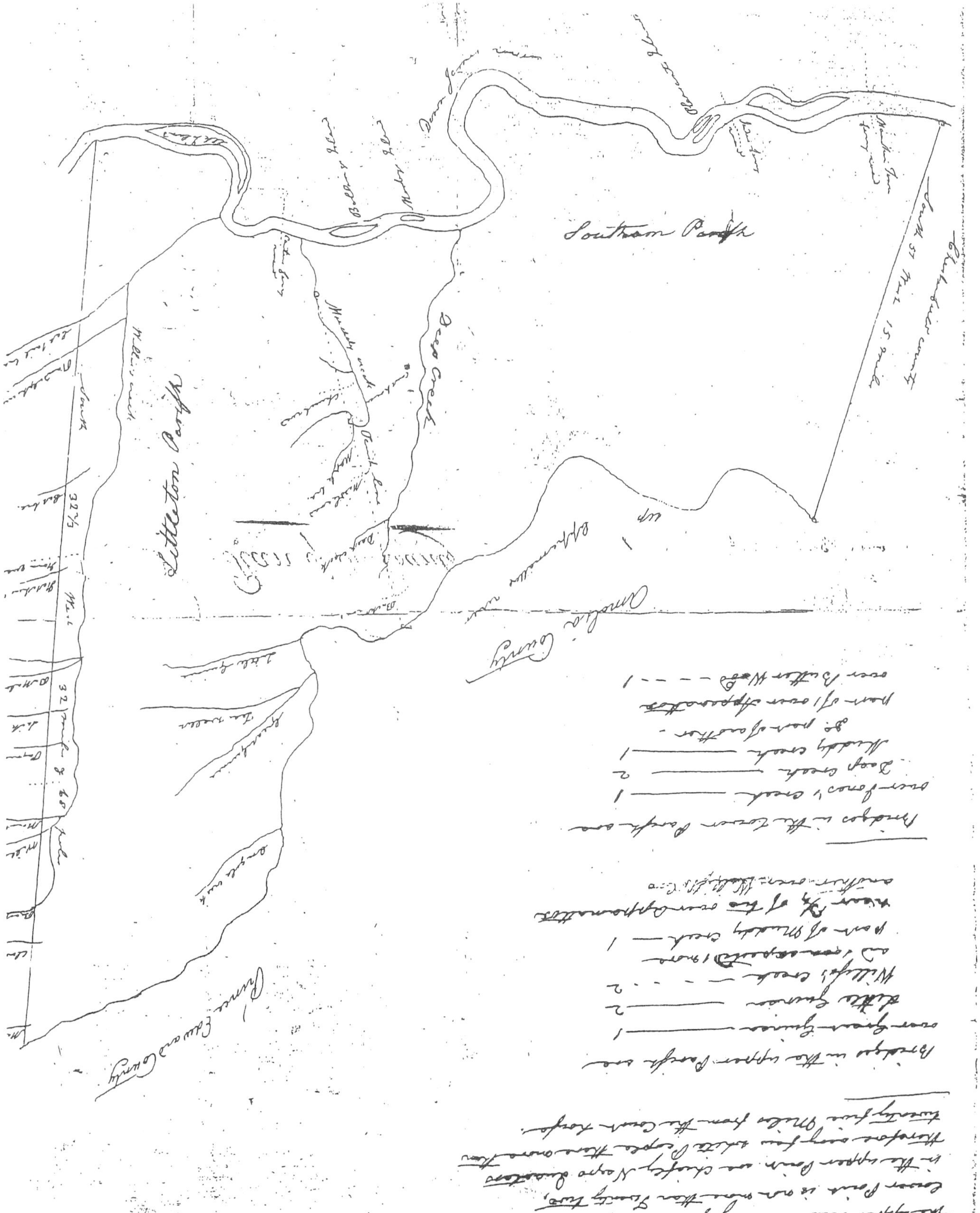
Southam Parish
Littleton Parish
Deep Creek
Amelia County
Prince Edward County
Cumberland County
South 57 West 15 miles

1858 VMI Cadet Map of Powhatan County

1864 Gilmer Map of Cumberland County

Map by permission of the Virginia Historical Society

1864 Gilmer Map of Powhatan County

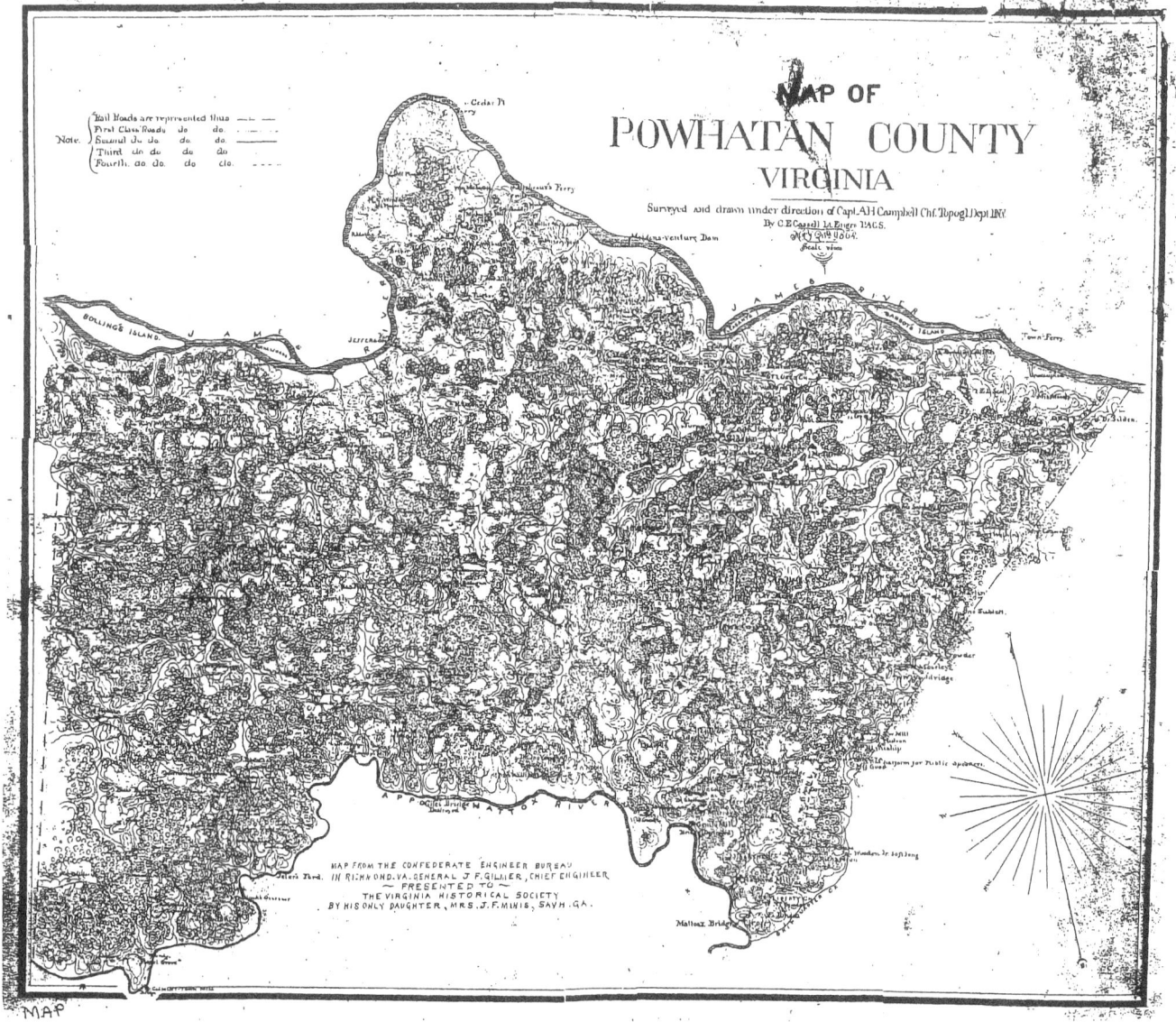

Map by permission of the Virginia Historical Society

1880 J. E. LaPrade Map of Powhatan County

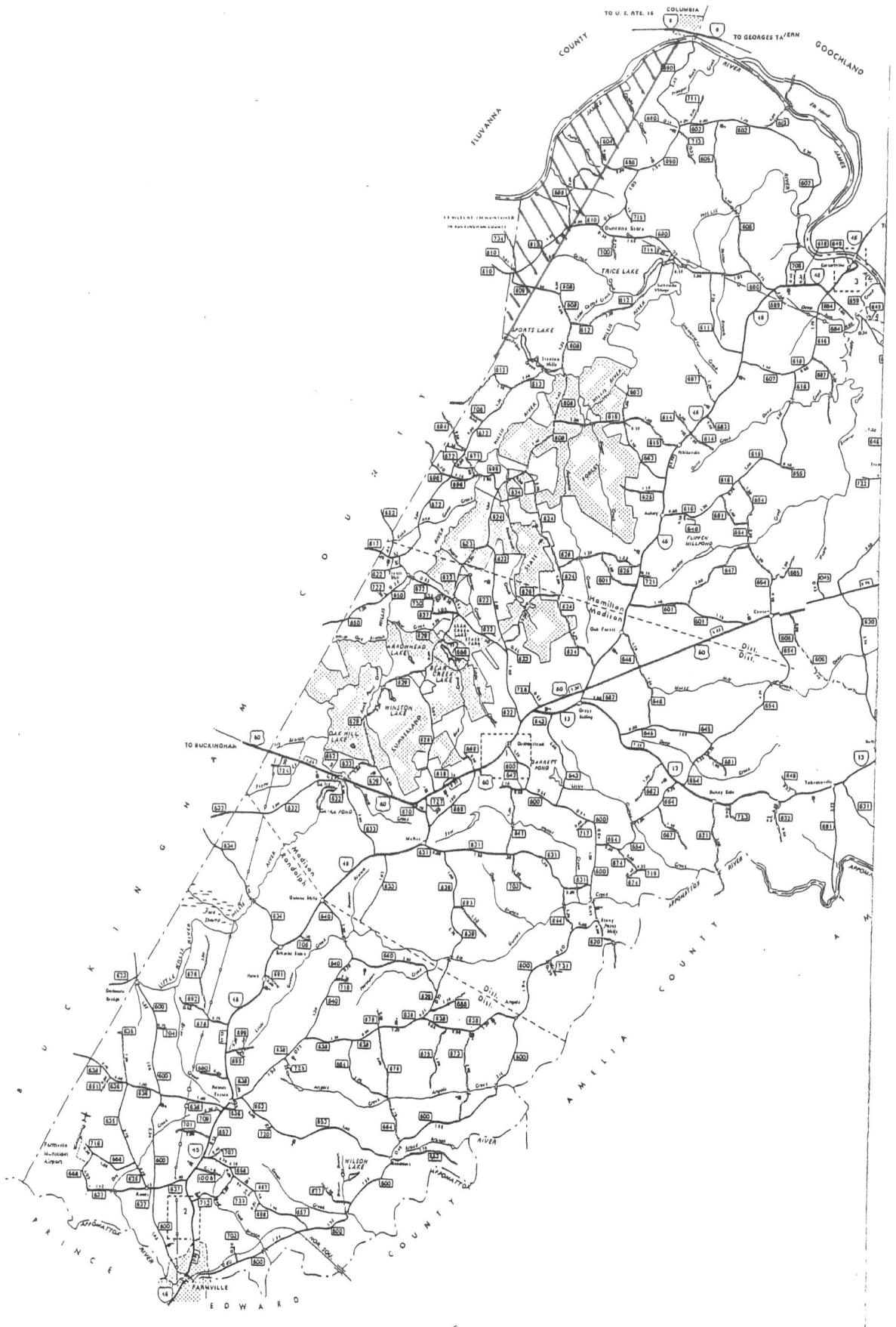

Modern Map of Southam Parish
Combination of Cumberland and Powhatan Counties

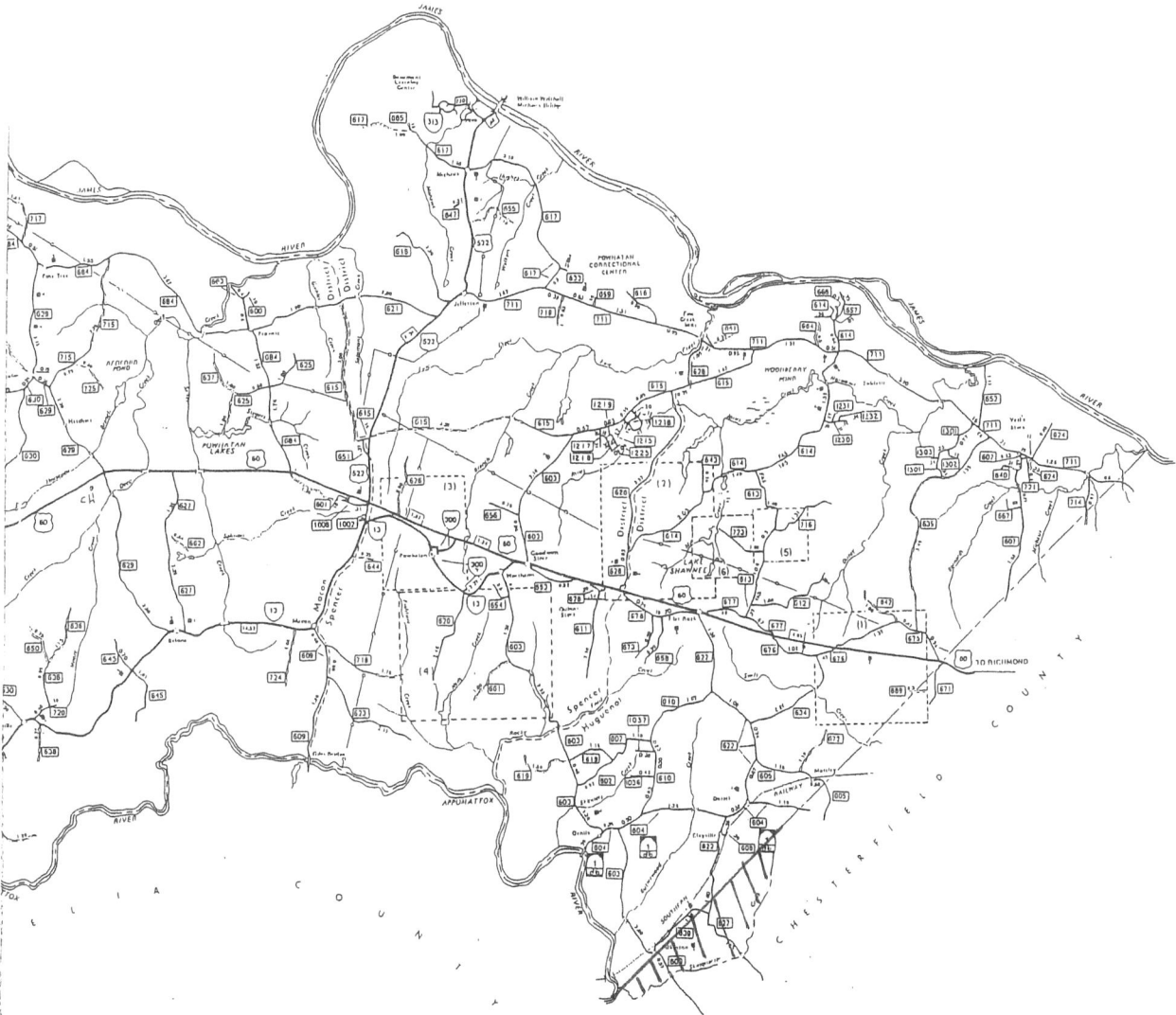

Modern Map of Southam Parish
Powhatan County

BIBLIOGRAPHY

BOOKS

Acts of the General Assembly of the State of Virginia, 1893.

Blomquist, Ann. *The Vestry Book of Southam Parish, Cumberland County, Virginia 1745-1792*. Willow Bend Books, 2002.

Cabell, Priscilla H. *Turff & Twigg, Volume One, The French Lands*. Richmond, VA, 1988.

Chamberlayne, C. G. *The Vestry Book of St. Paul's Parish 1706-1786*. Richmond, VA: The Library Board, 1940.

Cocke, Charles F. *Parish Lines, Diocese of Southern Virginia*. Richmond, VA: Library of Virginia, 1964.

Couture, Richard. *Powhatan: A Bicentennial History*. Richmond VA: Dietz Press, 1980.

Hening, William W. *The Statutes at Large, Being a Collection of All the Laws of Virginia*. Richmond and Philadelphia, 1809-1823.

Hopkins, Garland E. *The Story of Cumberland County, Virginia*. Privately issued, Westchester, Virginia, 1942.

Pawlett, Nathaniel. *Goochland County Road Orders 1728-1744*. Charlottesville, VA: Virginia Highway and Transportation Research Council, 1975.

Swem, Earl. *Maps Relating to Virginia in the Virginia State Library*. Richmond VA: Virginia State Library, 1914.

Tunis, Edwin. *Shaw's Fortune, The Picture Story of a Colonial Plantation*. Cleveland: World Publishing Co., 1966.

Tunis, Edwin. *Colonial Living*. Cleveland: World Publishing Co., 1957.

Vaughan, Michael K. *Crucible and Cornerstone, A History of Cumberland County, Virginia*. Atlanta, GA, 1969.

MAPS

Cumberland County
    1777 Map: size 15 5/8 x 12 1/4"; restored in April 1947; original at the Library of Virginia.
    1864 Map: Gilmer Map, VA Historical Society.
    1987 Map: Cumberland County VA General Highway Map, VA Dept. of Transportation.
    1992 Map: Cumberland County VA.
    c2002 Map: Anderson & Associates, County of Cumberland VA.
Powhatan County
    1858 Map: "Drawn by Cadets M. B. Hardin and L. W. Reed, VMI cadets, class of 1858 "
    1864 Map: Gilmer Map, VA Historical Society.
    1880 Map: "Map of Powhatan County, VA, by J. E. LaPrade, 1880."
    1987 Map: Powhatan County VA General Highway Map, VA Dept. of Transportation.
Grundset, Eric. *Historical Boundary Atlas of Central Virginia*, 1999.

MICROFILM

Vestry Book of Southam Parish, Miscellaneous Record 2288 (Accession 37796), Library of Virginia.

INDEX

Names often appear multiple times on a page. Also check alternate spellings.

Adams, Patrick   8
Adams, James   43
Agee, Matthew   3
Aiken, James   34
Aiken, see Akin
Akin, Isham   21,31,42
Akin, William   2,31,42
Akins, see Akin
Alday, Perrin   1
Alderson, Richard   43,55
Alexander   24
Alexander, John   5,13,46
Alford, Silvater   4,33
Allen, Archer   58
Allen, Archibald   58
Allen, Daniel   40,52
Allen, Francis   20,30,31
Allen, Isaac   12,19,40
Allen, James   12,19
Allen, James Sr   20
Allen, John   11
Allen, Joseph   52
Allen, Julius   20,25
Allen, Samuel Capt   11,22,32,35,43
Allen, Samuel Jr   7
Allen, Thomas   43
Allen, William   21,43,47,53
Amos, see Amoss
Amoss, Francis   26,54,58
Amoss, Francis Jr   47
Amoss, Francis Sr   47
Anderson   39
Anderson, Charles   11,19,29,39
Anderson, James   39,43,47
Anderson, Robert   47
Anderson, James   11,19,22,26,29
Andrews, Mark   40,43,52

Anglea, James   40
Anglea, Joseph   52
Anglea, William   19,20 40
Anglea, William Jr   30,40
Anglea, William Sr   40,52
Angola Creek   12,19,20,29,30,40,51,52
Appomattox River   1,2,7,8,11,12,13,19,20,
   21,22,29,30,31,32,36,39,40,41,42,51,52,
   53,54,61,63,64,65,67,68,70
Archdeacon, James   40
Archer, Field   68
Archer, Henry   66
Archer, John   2,8,33,39,44
Archer, William   31,64,66
Arms, Edward   46
Armstead, John   26,35,47,58
Arnold, Henry   12
Arnold, James   41
Arnold, Thomas   20
Arnold, William   12,20,30,40,41
Arnold, William Jr   40
Askew's Path   3
Atkins, Samuel   26
Atkins, Joseph   23
Atkinson, Samuel   47
Austin, Archer   41
Austin, James   58
Austin, William   48

Bagby, Henry   4,24,33,44,45,66
Bagby, James   45,66,69
Bagby, Robert   16,24,33,45
Bagby, William   66
Bailey, Abraham   22
Bailey, Benjamin   42
Bailey, William   13,19,21,29,31,41

Bowler, Ben 41
Bowlings Road 11
Bracket, Thomas 5,6
Bradley, David 12
Bradley, James 67
Bradley, John 5,11,15,22,43,47,54
Bradley, Thomas 3
Bradshaw, Charles 25
Bradshaw, Field 25
Bradshaw, John 25
Bradshaw, Josiah 25
Bradshaw, William 25
Bransford, James 64
Brazeal, Henry 2,13,21
Bridgewater, Samuel 6,14,26,47,58
Brooks' Mill 7,8
Brooks' Road 8,11,19,29,39,51
Brown, Davis 52
Brown, James 19,22,26,29,40,43,47,54,58
Brown, John 8,19,40,41,43,52
Brown, Robert 47,57
Brown, Samuel 26,47,58
Brown, Zachariah 19,40
Brumskil 43
Brumskil, John 25
Bryant, James 45
Buckingham Road 1,2,3,6,7,8,11,12,13,15,
    16,21,22,23,25,26,30,31,32,33,35,36,41,
    42,43,44,47,52,53,54,55,57,61,62,63,64,
    65,67,68,69,70
Bullock, John 22,43
Burch, John 33,44
Burford, Milton 47
Burnett, John 6,26
Burton 31, 53
Burton, Hutchins 7, 8
Burton, John 20,22,25,32,41,43,47,52,54,
    55,65
Burton, Josiah 7
Burton, Richard 7
Burton, Robert 7,26
Burton, Samuel 7,8,21
Burton, William 41

Burton, William A. 67
Burton's Brook 41,53
Burton's Creek 52
Burton's Ordinary 43
Burton's Path 8
Butler, Aaron 29,39
Butler, Joseph 26
Butler, Orphans 47
Butterwood Creek 1

Caesor, see Seizer
Calland, Joseph 39,40,51,52,54
Calwell, Thomas 54
Campbell, Peter 43
Cannefax, John 2,16,33
Cannon, Benjamin 26, 36
Cannon, Jeremiah 36,48
Cannon, John 4
Cardwell, George 16,23,44
Cardwell, John 7,15,46
Cardwell, Richard 15
Carner, Susannah 33
Carr, William 24,66
Carrington, George 2,5,6,26,36,46,47,48
Carrington, John 44
Carrington, Paul 36
Carter, Daniel 23
Carter, Jesse 41,53,63
Carter, John 14,25,26,46,47
Carter, John Jr 47
Carter, Robert 5,6,26,48
Carter, Robert Jr 5,14,25,26
Carter, Thomas 6,40
Carter's Ferry Road 35,46,47,56,57,58
Cary, Archibald 8,11,26,29,35,39,43,47,
    51,54
Chafin, Christopher 20,40
Chafin, John 12, 20
Chafin, Joseph 52
Chafin, Nathan 52
Chafin, Stanley 52
Chair Road 6,7,15,25

Cox, George 8,12,21,31,41,53,63,67
Cox, Hall 21,31
Cox, Henry 8,31,41,63,67
Cox, Henry Jr 41
Cox, Henry Sr 67
Cox, John 4,26,31,41,42,44,45,56,61,62,
   66,69
Cox, Joseph 41
Cox, Judith 41
Cox, Nicholas 3,25
Cox, Stephen 7,8,13
Cox, William 6,24,33,44,45,66,67
Cox's Mill 41,53
Crafford, James 24
Creasy, John 5,35,46
Creeks, see each one
   Angola, Burton's, Butterwood, Deep,
   Fighting, Fine, Green, Jones, Little, Great
   Guinea, Little Guinea, Mill, Muddy,
   Randolph's, Randolph's Mill, Soakass,
   Solomon's, Swann's, Tearwallet
Criddle, Allen 58
Cross Road 53
Crump, Richard 67
Cumpton, Richard 66
Cunningham, Alexander 26
Cunningham, James 5,6,26,36
Cunningham, James Jr 14
Cunningham, Jonathan 14,26
Cunningham, William 6

Daniel 7,8,32,43,54
Daniel, Edward 14
Daniel, Hezekiah 56
Daniel, James 6,8,11,19,20,43,58
Daniel, John 43
Daniel, Richard 20,21,30,31
Daniel, Walter 7
Daniel, Walthoe 47
Daniel, Watt 26
Daniel, Williams 8,11,20,22,32,41,43,54,
   63,67

Davenport 40
Davenport, Capt 41
Davenport, Henry 20,30
Davenport, James 20,30
Davenport, Joseph 30,41
Davenport, Julius 29,39
Davenport, Mary 41
Davenport, Philemon 30
Davenport, Stephen 30
Davenport, Thomas 8,39,51,52
Davenport, Thomas Jr 20,30
Davenport, Thomas Sr 20,41
Davenport, William 30,40,41,52
Daverson, Hezekiah 48
Davidson, Edward 12
Davies, Nicholas 5,14,24,34,46
Davies, Henry Landon 56
Davis, Charles 13
Davis, George 42,44,53,61,64,68
Davis, James 2,3,13,16,23,42,44
Davis, William 12,33,44,45
Davison, David 19
Davison, Hezekiah 57
Davison, William 19
Day, Peter 64
Dean, John 64
Deep Creek 3,13,14,15,23,24,25,26,34,41,
   45,46,56,57,58,62,63,66,67,69,70
Deep Creek Bridge 5
Depp, Peter 65
Dews, Thomas 47
Dickens, Christopher 26
Dickens, Thomas 4
Dickerson, David 52
Diggs, Dudley 4
Dillon, Benjamin 47
Dillon, Henry 5,14,25,26,46
Dillon, Widow 14,25,26
Dillon, William 5,26,46,47
Dorham, James 40
Doss, Joshua 19,52
Doudy, James 8
Douglas, Robert 6,35,46

Furlong, Robert 46

Gaddy, George 45
Gamon, John 31
Gannaway, John 29
Gannaway, John Sr 51
Garden, Parson 58
Gardian, James 47
Garrett, James 54
Garrett, Henry 22,43,54
Gasper, Susannah 4,16
Gathwrite, Miles 5
Gay, Elizabeth 45
Gay, William 66
Genito Bridge 12,13
Genito Road 1,21,22,31,32,42,53,54,61,64,
   65,68
Giles, Nicholas 2,21,31
Gilliam, James 36,47,48,57
Gilliam, Joseph 48
Gladoe, Samuel 22
Glass, James 4
Glebe 3,24,45
Glen, see Glenn
Glenn, Gideon 8,20,40,52
Glenn, James 20,52
Glenn, James Sr 52
Glenn, Nathan 40, 52
Glenn, Nehemiah 12,20,30,52
Glenn's Path 20,30,40,52
Glover, John 47
Glover, Joseph 48
Glover, Phineas 6,14,26,36,47,48
Glover, Phineas Jr 57
Glown, James 52
Going, George 5,13
Goode, Benjamin 2
Goode, Bennet 16,23,33,44,56,62,66,69
Goode, John 62,69
Gordon, Robert 67
Great Deep Creek Bridge 6
Great Guinea Creek 3,8,11,12,20,30,40,52

Green Creek 8,19,29,39,40,51
Griffin, Joseph 48
Grisham 39
Guinea Road 12,20,30,31,41,52,53
Guttery, Alexander 54
Guttery, Bernard 52
Guttery, Thomas 11,22,32,43
Guttery, William 54

Hadaway, David 8
Hale, John 2
Hales, John 13
Hall, Robert 29
Hall, Thomas 1,2,13
Hall, William 29
Ham Chapel 5,6,14,25,26,58
Hamblet, Thomas 21
Hambleton, Edward 6,26
Hambleton, William 20,30, 40, 41, 52
Hammon, Ambrose 19
Hammon, John Sr 19
Hammon, Joseph 40
Hancock, George 22,32
Hancock, Margaret 1
Hanson 44
Harman, Henry 12,20,30,40,43
Harrelson, John 22
Harris, Ann 67
Harris, Benjamin 6,7,8,22,32,43
Harris, Charles 64
Harris, Edward 67,70
Harris, Francis E 67,70
Harris, Joseph 55,63,67,70
Harris' Mill Path 36
Harris' Path 15,23,41
Harris, Thomas 12
Harrison, Benjamin 5,6,7,11,14,15,22,26,
   35,47
Harrison, Carter 26,47
Harrison, Carter Henry 46,47,56
Harrison, Orphans 47
Harrison's Road 11,15,22,32,35,43,47,54

Word, Thomas   51
Worley, John   1,3,31,42
Worley, William   1,2,31,42,44
Worley's Chapel   1,13
Wright, Ambrose   39,40
Wright, George   11,19,29,39,51,52
Wright, Griffin   52
Wright, John   7,19,29,40,52
Wright, Paul   66
Wright, Thomas   40,52

Yarbrough   21

ABOUT THE AUTHOR

Ann K. Blomquist is a high school mathematics teacher whose genealogy pursuits include writing and historical clothing. When she makes presentations about her books, she wears reproduction clothing to demonstrate the era of the book. Ms. Blomquist has more than 30 years experience as a family genealogist in Southern research, and has published numerous books including: *The Vestry Book of Southam Parish, Cumberland County, Virginia, 1745-1792*; *Cheek's Cross Road, Tennessee, Store Account Book, 1802-1807*; *The Cruel War, The Civil War Letters of Grant and Malinda Taylor, Pickens County, Alabama*; *Taylors and Tates of the South*; *Kickers of the South*; *The 40th Alabama Infantry, Confederate States Army*; and *The Mill Account Journal of Jeremiah M. Tate, Pickens County, Alabama, 1873-1875*.

www.ingramcontent.com/pod-product-compliance
Lightning Source LLC
Chambersburg PA
CBHW081157270326
41930CB00014B/3186